HOW TO FIND YOUR JOY
AND PURPOSE

FOUR EASY STEPS TO DISCOVER A JOB YOU WANT
AND LIVE THE LIFE YOU LOVE

CASSANDRA GAISFORD

HANNAH JOY

This book is dedicated to love.
And to those struggling to find or sustain their joy,
And to all our clients
who have shared their joy and purpose with us,
and allowed us to help make their dreams come true.
Thank you
for inspiring us.

CONTENTS

HOW TO FIND YOUR JOY AND PURPOSE:

Cassandra Gaisford, BCA, Dip Psych
Hannah Joy, BCom.

PRAISE FOR HOW TO FIND YOUR JOY AND PURPOSE

"This is really, really good! A wonderful and inspiring book. LOVE it! It's concise, personal and practical. I can think of so many people who could benefit from this book."

~ Heather Dodge, Founder Kaleidoscope Solutions

"How to Find Your Joy and Purpose is a practical guide, with thought-provoking realistic tools that guided me on a journey of discovery, learning me. It is easy reading, practical and from the heart. It is written for me and speaks to me—which is how any self-help/improvement book should be. I loved the book!"

~ Joanna Baldwin

"My takeaway is that the power is within me to navigate through the dark periods and emerge, empowered and capable of managing my emotions, moods, and those dips in life. And I can do this without need to access outside of myself, which is an amazing gift. Broken down in manageable steps, it's achievable! :) *How to Find Your Joy and*

Purpose was very thorough. A reflection of Cassandra's extensive experience and Hannah's recent, very fresh, experience in re-finding her joy. Loved it."

~ **Jamie S.**

AUTHORS NOTE

"WE WROTE THIS BOOK BECAUSE WE NEEDED TO READ IT."

We're feeling joyful as we collaborate, as mother and daughter, on our first book together, *How to Find Your Joy and Purpose: Four Easy Steps to Discover A Job You Want And Live the Life You Love.*

This is a particularly significant project for us, as you'll discover. We're writing at a time of great personal upheaval and turmoil. Over an abruptly short period of time we realized that we had lost our joy. We were burned out and stressed out. And it seemed as though the world had become more toxic, selfish, and meaner. We had been following our passions, but life didn't seem to be flowing.

Wasn't it supposed to get easier?

Follow your bliss, we were told, and shared with others. What we didn't heed, was the need to keep our vibrations high and prioritize self-care.

Everything got better for us when we began to make peace with the fact that it might never get easier. The world can be crazy-busy. WE CAN BE CRAZY-BUSY.

Life is a great teacher, sometimes brutally so, but the lessons are enduring ones.

Whether you are burned out, stressed out, blissed-out or checked out, the question is always the same: How do you find your joy and purpose and keep it without crashing or sacrificing your mental health?

This book is a list of things that have helped us. We wrote to heal ourselves and in the process of recovery we discovered how extraordinarily powerful everyday joy is.

We learned how simple, quick and effective joy can be in healing so many of the things facing humanity. Depression, anxiety, stress, lack of meaning and purpose, toxic careers and unhappiness at work, abhorrent rates of suicide and addiction, acute loneliness and more.

We wrote *How to Find Your Joy and Purpose* primarily for anyone trying to create and sustain a meaningful, healthy, and prosperous life. Whether you are a homemaker, retiree, entrepreneur, artist, employee, activist, career-changer or simply looking for a lift this book is for you.

There are no hard and speedy rules, of course—life is an art, not a science. Your route may vary. Pack what you need and leave the rest.

Hang on to hope, follow your joy, keep going, and take care of your beautiful self—mentally, emotionally, physically, and spiritually.

We'll do the same.

INTRODUCTION

"We need joy as we need air. We need love as we need water. We need each other as we need the earth we share."
Maya Angelou

Joy is the truth. The whole truth. And always our truth. Without joy we lack vitality. Without vitality we have lethargy.

Finding a job you want and living a life you love is impossible without joy, purpose, passion, enthusiasm, zest, inspiration and the deep satisfaction that comes from doing something that delivers you some kind of zing.

Yet, it's staggeringly, and dishearteningly, true that many people don't know what fills them with joy, or how they can channel it into an enriching life and rewarding career. Some research suggests that only 10% of people are living and working with joy.

Many people feel trapped and frustrated. People like Tom, an estate planning attorney in the US, who wrote to Cassandra, "I have spent 29 years as an attorney, mostly unhappy, but it's hard to get out. I still do not know my passion. I have some ideas, but I am not sure which 1 or 2 will cause me to jump out of bed at 5:30 a.m., drink a lot of coffee and eat a few biscuits and begin my mission."

If you're like many people who don't know what they feel joyful, passionate, or purposeful about or what gives your life meaning and purpose, this book will help provide the answers.

If you have been told it's not realistic to work and live with joy, this book will help change your mindset.

If you're recovering from burnout, washout or timeout, *How to Find Your Joy and Purpose* comes to your rescue.

Together we'll help you get your mojo back, challenge your current beliefs and increase your sense of possibility. By tapping into a combination of practical strategies, Law of Attraction principles, and the spiritual powers of manifestation, you'll reawaken dreams, boost your self-awareness, empower your life and challenge what you thought was possible.

We'll do this in an inspired, yet structured way, by strengthening your creative thinking skills, boosting your self-awareness and helping you identify your non-negotiable ingredients for career success and happiness.

Little steps will lead naturally to bigger leaps, giving you the courage and confidence to follow your joy and purpose and fly free towards career happiness and life fulfillment. All while keeping your sanity!

What you're about to read isn't another self-help book; it's a self-empowerment book. It offers ways to increase your self-knowledge. From that knowledge comes the power to create a life worth living.

How to Find Your Joy and Purpose will help you:

- Explore and clarify your joys, passion, interests, and life purpose
- Build a strong foundation for happiness and success
- Value your gifts, and talents and confirm your natural knacks and work-related strengths
- Direct your energies positively toward your preferred future
- Strengthen your creative thinking skills, and ability to

identify possible roles you would enjoy, including self-employment and enriching hobbies
- Have the courage to follow your dreams and super-charge the confidence needed to make an inspired change
- Find your point of brilliance

Let's look briefly at what each chapter in this book will cover:

Step One, "The Call For Joy" will help you explore the meaning of joy and discover the benefits of following it, and consequences of ignoring your joy. You'll identify any blocking beliefs and intensify joy-building beliefs to boost your chances of success.

Step Two, "Discover Your Joy," will help you to identify your own sources of joy and joy criteria. What you'll discover may be a complete surprise and open up a realm of opportunities you've never considered.

Step Three, "Joy at Work," will assist you in identifying career options and exploring ways to develop your career in light of your joy and life purpose.

Step Four, "Live Your Joy," looks at joy beyond the world of work and ways to achieve greater balance and fulfillment. You'll also identify strategies to overcome obstacles and maximize your success.

How to Find Your Joy and Purpose concludes with showing you how to identify your point of brilliance.

THIS BOOK IS MAGICAL

This book proves less really is more. Sometimes all it takes to radically transform your life is one word, one sentence, one powerful but simple strategy to ignite inspiration and reawaken a sense of possibility.

We have successfully used the knowledge we're sharing with you in this book professionally with our clients and personally during numerous reinventions—including recovering from recent trauma.

We stand by every one of the 4 steps and the 50+ strategies you will learn here, not just because they are grounded in strong evidence-based, scientific and spiritual principles, but also because we have successfully used them to create turnaround, after turnaround in nearly every area of our life.

How to Find Your Joy and Purpose is the culmination of all that we have experienced and all that we have learned, applied and taught others for decades. We don't practice what we preach; we preach what we have practiced—because it gets results.

WHY DID WE WRITE THIS BOOK?

As we shared in the Authors Note, after experiencing a period of extreme stress and burnout we both crashed. For Hannah Joy, neglecting self-care, over-working and discovering a historical trauma that had lain buried in the subconscious for over 23 years careered to the surface in a violent storm.

Her life was busy, busy, busy. Too busy. She was running her business full-time, studying with other coaches, attending numerous workshops on personal development—and leading others. Plus, she was part way through a full-time tertiary course to qualify as a counselor.

Add to that the trauma of discovering that her partner of four years had been cheating on her, it's no wonder she flipped out. Like many people, she turned to alcohol to help her cope. Following binge-drinking 3/4 of a bottle of Jack Daniel's, Tennessee whiskey, in one session she was lucky she didn't die. Instead she suffered alcohol-induced psychosis and rather, be taken somewhere safe to sober up, she was admitted into psychiatric care and medicated.

We'll share more of Hannah story in a book Hannah is writing, but suffice to say we quickly discovered how truly broken and antiquated the mental health system is. Pharmaceuticals may offer a bridge to healing but seldom cures—particularly when the real issue is sexual assault trauma and alcohol harm.

We were both significantly progressed on our spiritual paths, and valued a holistic approach—something at odds with The System.

While struggling from the outside to help her daughter (then 'owned' by The State) Cassandra struggled to reach her. She couldn't even bring her home.

Cassandra began to think, What would our life be like if we just leaned toward joy? This question led us to what Cassandra calls a *da-Vinci* and *to* conduct our own experiment.

As part of Hannah's journey to recovery Cassandra asked her to write a chapter of this book—something that would help Hannah with whatever she was going through at the time.

And we began to measure our success based on how Hannah's feelings of hopelessness and disempowerment and fear changed.

At the same time, Cassandra wrote chapters that would help her. If you've ever supported anyone though a mental health crisis, or saved them from acting out suicidal thoughts, or loved someone who is suffering (often brutally so), you'll know you suffer too.

Hannah and I went on a quest for joy and purpose. We began looking for joy in trauma, seeking purpose in suffering, and going out of our way to seek joy in all situations—especially the more difficult areas of our life.

We began questioning addictive over-working, mindlessly drinking, blurring boundaries, and escaping healing by numbing and distraction. Instead we opted to test-drive new hobbies and laughing at our own worry-minded thinking.Hannah has a new passion for crochet and Cassandra has taken up jewelry making!

Whenever we'd notice ourselves getting stuck in a negative story, we'd challenge ourselves to be the heroine of our own story and fastfroward to a new scene. Or simply try to rescript the story and see it with the high-vibe perspective of joy.

We'd say to ourselves, "What if we just chose joy? What if we just did this for fun? What if we just allowed." Asking ourselves these questions, and others you'll find in this book, in any given moment immediately catapulted us back into a place of joy.

HOW TO USE THIS BOOK

This book is a concise guide to making the most of your life. The vision was simple: a few short, easy to digest tips for time-challenged people who were looking for inspiration and practical strategies to encourage positive change.

From our own experience, we knew that people didn't need a large wad of words to feel inspired, gain clarity and be stimulated to take action.

In this era of information obesity the need for simple, life-affirming messages is even more important. If you are looking for inspiration and practical tips, in short, sweet sound bites, this guide is for you.

Similarly, if you are a grazer, or someone more methodical, this guide will also work for you. Pick a page at random, or work through the steps sequentially. We encourage you to experiment, be open-minded and try new things. We promise you will achieve outstanding results.

Clive, a 62-year-old man who had suffered work-related burnout, did! He thought that creating a journal, *Tip 14* in this guide, was childish—something other stressed executives in his men's support group would balk at. But once he'd taken up the challenge he told me enthusiastically, "They loved it!" They are using their journals to visualize, gain clarity, and create their preferred futures. Clive used it to help manifest his new purpose-driven coaching business.

Let experience be your guide. Give your brain a well-needed break. Let go of 'why', and embrace how you *feel*, or how you want to feel. Honor the messages from your intuition and follow your path with heart.

Laura, who at one stage seemed rudderless career-wise, did just that. She was guided to *Tip 21: Who Inspires You?* Following that, her motivation to live and work like those she looked up to sparked a determination to start her own business. It was that simple. And now she's done it!

HOW TO USE THIS BOOK—YOUR VIRTUAL COACH

To really benefit from this book think of it as your 'virtual' coach— answer the questions and complete the additional exercises included in each chapter.

Questions are great thought provokers. Your answers to these questions will help you gently challenge current assumptions and gain greater clarity about your goals and desires.

All the strategies are designed to facilitate greater insight and to help you integrate new learnings. Resist the urge to just process information in your head. We learn best by doing. Research has repeatedly proven that the act of writing deepens your knowledge and understanding.

For example, a study conducted by Dr. David K. Pugalee, found that journal writing was an effective instructional tool and aided learning. His research found that writing helped people organize and describe internal thoughts and thus improve their problem solving-skills.

Henriette Klauser, Ph.D., also provides compelling evidence in her book, *Write It Down and Make It Happen*, that writing helps you clarify what you want and enables you to make it happen.

Writing down your insights is the area where people like motivational guru Tony Robbins, say that the winners part from the losers, because the losers always find a reason not to write things down. Harsh but perhaps true!

KEEPING A JOY JOURNAL

A joy journal is also a great place to store sources of inspiration to support you through the career planning and change process. For some tips to help you create your own inspirational joy journal, go to Cassandra's media page on her website and watch her television interview and interview with other experts here:

http://www.cassandragaisford.com/media

SETTING YOU UP FOR SUCCESS

"Aren't you setting people up for failure?" a disillusioned career coach once challenged Cassandra.

Thirty-five years of cumulative professional experience as a career coach and holistic therapist, helping people work with joy and purpose and still pay the bills, answers that question. Cassandra is setting people up for success. We're not saying it will happen instantly, but if you follow the advice in this book, it will happen.

We promise.

We've proven repeatedly, both personally and professionally, that thinking differently and creatively, rationally and practically, while also harnessing the power of your heart, and applying the principles of manifestation, really works. In this book, we'll show you why —and how.

A large part of our philosophy and the reason behind our success with clients is our fervent belief that to achieve anything worthy of life you need to follow your joy. And we're in good company.

As trauma survivor and media giant Oprah Winfrey once said, "I define joy as a sustained sense of well-being and internal peace—a connection to others."

JOY'S PAY CHEQUE

By discovering your joy and purpose you will tap into a huge source of potential energy and prosperity. Pursuing your joy can be profitable on many levels:

- When you do what you love, your true talent will reveal itself; joy can't be faked
- You'll be more enthusiastic about your pursuits
- You'll have more energy to overcome obstacles
- You will be more determined to make things happen
- You will enjoy your work
- Your work will become a vehicle for self-expression
- Joy will give you a competitive edge
- You'll enjoy your life and magnetize positive experiences toward you
- Your find eternal peace

Without joy, you don't have connection to what truly matters, and without connection you are alone.

Let the higher vibrations of joy, peace, love, desire, purpose and passion lift you higher. Allow this higher energy to lift fear, ambivalence, apathy and negativity.

Don't waste another day feeling uninspired. Don't be the person who spends a life of regret, or waits until they retire before they follow their joy, be you. Don't be the person too afraid to make a change for the better, or who wishes they could lead a significant life. Make the change now. Before it's too late.

Reach For Your Dreams

Joy, fulfillment, passion, purpose, peace and love—call it what you will, our deepest desire is that this book encourages you to reach for your dreams, to never settle, to believe in the highest aspirations you have for yourself.

You have so many gifts, so many talents that the world so desperately needs. We need people like you who care about what they do, who want to live and work with joy and purpose.

And what we can promise you is this—whatever your circumstances, it's never too late to re-create yourself and your life. So, what are you waiting for?

Let's get started!

STEP 1: THE CALL FOR JOY

Read through the following tips numbered 1-12 and consider your responses to each strategy. You may want to keep notes about your responses in a special book or journal.

Tips 1-12 ask you to consider what you believe joy is and to identify what joy means to you. What role do you think joy should have in your life? Do you have any joy-blocking beliefs? What are your joy-building beliefs?

What are the the consequences of ignoring your joy? How do you think not pursuing your dreams might affect you? How has it affected other people you know? What are your goals, hopes, and dreams for your future? What will having more joy in your life do for you?

WHAT IS JOY?

"The two most inspiring life forces are anger and joy – I could
write 6 zillion songs about these two feelings alone."
Alanis Morissette

Joy is energy.
Joy is a feeling.
Joy is about emotion.
Joy is one of the highest vibrations we can experience.
Joy is about delight and rapture.
Joy is about jubilation, elation, euphoria, and exultation.
Joy is about eagerness and preoccupation.
Joy is about excitement, animation, and delight.
Joy is about triumph, conscious cultivation, and choice.
Joy is peace and transcendence.
Joy is being wholehearted.
Joy is love.

Joy is many things. What is joy to you?

JOY FOR ALL

"'Where is my soul?' That is perhaps the only question worth
answering. Each of us answers in his or her own way."
Piero Ferrucci

Every human being is capable of joy. Different people are joyful in
different ways and about different things.

Many people think that being joyful only means being loud and
extraverted.

This isn't true at all. Many joyful people are contained, or quiet or
reserved. Joyful people come in all shapes, sizes, and ages. You can
pursue your joy at any age and stage of your life. You can even choose
to be joyful in the face of great difficulty.

Where is your soul? How does joy show up for you?

WHAT CAN JOY DO?

"Joy is something different from happiness. When I use the word happiness, in a sense I mean satisfaction. Sometimes we have a painful experience, but that experience, as you've said with birth, can bring great satisfaction and joyfulness."
His Holiness The Dalai Lama

Joy energizes people.
Joy inspires people.
Joy helps people lead happier lives.
Joy is an indispensable part of feeling alive.
Joy helps us overcome difficulties.
Joy liberates us. It frees us to be ourselves.
Joy opens up fresh horizons.
Joy is fabulous for our health.

When we are pursuing something we are enthusiastic about our energy, drive and determination is infinite. Our courage and resilience soars and we are able to stretch to anything, accommodate any setback, and bounce forward again.

People immobilized by fear and passivity snap like twigs.
Joy is the light of balance for those of us seeking a way out of the darkness of depression and suffering. Joy gives us a zing in our soul, a reason for living and the confidence, tenacity, and drive to pursue our dreams.

Record all the reasons why you want more joy in your life. What would you do if you were 10 times joyful?

What are all the benefits that will flow?

REALITY CHECK ON JOY

"Everyone seeks happiness, joyfulness, but from outside—from money, from power, from big car, from big house. Most people never pay much attention to the ultimate source of a happy life, which is inside, not outside."
His Holiness, The Dalai Lama

Joy does not always come easily. Life is challenging—sometimes overwhelmingly so. Like anything worthwhile, finding and following your joy often involves great commitment, courage, and sacrifice.

Joyful people are prepared to give up things they once enjoyed or people they may have endured to live a more peaceful life. They're prepared to wave bye-bye to addictions that keep them boringly distracted, disconnected, or toxically numbed. They commit daily to waving farewell to deep diving into narcissism, drama, and negativity.

They affirm with joy 'yes' to letting go of pain, fear, and judgment. 'Yes' to embracing unconditional love, vulnerability, taking risks and coping with the possibility of failure. "Yes!Yes!Yes! To embracing their essence and being who they truly are.

Joyful people aren't always chasing 'happy.' Contribution, compassion, and caring—for self and others—are more important virtues.

The compensation for being 'real' is a bigger, richer, more authentically fulfilling life.

What are you prepared to trade-off to be more joyful? What are you prepared to change in your life? What or who would help you? What or who would stop you?

5

COMPARISON ROBS JOY

"Comparison is the thief of joy."
Theodore Roosevelt

Constantly thinking what others are doing, stalking others on social media, and berating yourself for feeling inadequate in comparison drains your energy and robs your joy. Yet it can be addictive.

Like any addiction again it's a harmful habit if taken to extremes, Comparison can be self sabotaging and a form of self abuse. It's also a hard pattern to stop. But stop you must if your joy it is to be returned to you.

We're curious, social beings. We are drawn to others, we like to know what people are up to, and we like to follow successful people.

But we don't see everyone's entire life.We only see one glance—and often it's a carefully curated one.

We don't befriend ourselves enough and acknowledge our difficult journey, and how we have triumphed over trauma, or how far we've come. Some of what we have experienced others may never have experienced—much less survived.

Instead of comparing ourselves to others negatively, to reclaim joy we need to think about where we are now and compare this to where we have been—yesterday, last week, last month, last year. This is especially important when we are recovering for illness or a setback of any kind. Traumatic experiences or mental health challenges can make us especially vulnerable.

Use aspirational comparisons. Compare yourself to people similar to you or who have been in the same spot and are now flourishing. Think of someone you aspire to be like. Oprah? Drew Barrymore? Your mother? Or a dear friend?

Surround yourself with your mentors People who are inspiring and smile in the face of adversity are like vitamins for our souls.

Look back at a time you felt joy and compare yourself to that person. But be careful you don't hold onto the old you and forget to feed the new emerging you.

YOUR BODY BAROMETER

"We store memories in our bodies. We store passion and heartache. We store joy, moments of transcendent peace. If we are to access these, if we are to move into them and through them, we must enter our bodies."
Julia Cameron

Our bodies are storytellers. Like any great story, there are chapters with villains and heroes, plot twists, hidden dangers and deeper truths within the layers.

Our storytelling body never lies, however, many people soldier on ignoring the obvious warning signs their body is narrating.

When you don't do the things you love your health can suffer. Common signs of neglecting your joy and purpose can include, headaches, insomnia, tiredness, depression, anger, frustration, and irritability.

It's easy to ignore or rationalize the feelings of discomfort, but the reality is your body—and your soul—is screaming out to be saved.

When we enter our bodies, we enter our hearts. We tap into our

DNA, or genetic code. Our DNA is the antenna of our body, broadcasting epiphanies, and announcing breakthroughs in the tight fabric of fear and frustration.

Pay heed as it measures the heights of your joy, the peaks of your passion, and feel the smile on your face as you finally understand that the pathway to joy and the divine intelligence within has always been open and available to you. If you will listen.

Our DNA orchestrates our cellular structure to enhance who we are, and to complement our life. It tells us when we are settling and when we are honoring the Mastery within. It uses each layer of its own magnificence in the perfect ways that will create the balm of healing, a confluence of love creation, and an honoring of our soul's intent.

Our bodies want us to rejoice, which is why increasing awareness is being placed on body-based therapies for sustained health and healing.

When you feel unfulfilled, or frustrated where and what do you notice in your body? How does this differ from times when you are joyful?

What would it take to have the courage to say 'enough' and pursue more satisfying alternatives?

NO REGRETS

"If you bring forth what is within you, what you bring forth will save you. If you do not bring forth what is within you, what you do not bring forth will destroy you."
Gospel of Thomas

A life of no regret—isn't that what we all want? Some people, who in their hearts know that they are capable of much more, never pursue their heart's desire.

A study by Cornwell University, published in *Emotion* confirmed that three elements make up our sense of self: the actual, the ought, and the ideal selves.

The actual self is made up of the attributes we believe we possess; the ought self is the person we feel we should have been, based on our obligations and responsibilities; the ideal self are the attributes, such as hopes, goals, aspirations, dreams and wishes, we would ideally like to possess.

Abraham Maslow theorized in his infamous hierarchy of needs that becoming a self actualized person was the driving ambition and purpose of life. The ultimate success, he claimed, was to be all that we are capable of becoming.

Regret is a feeling of sorrow or remorse. Regret because of stagnation, not growing, and chasing the wrong dreams is a major source of depression, stress, and anger for many people.

True joy is living an unregrettable life swimming in an energy of abundance. The word affluence means 'to flow in abundance' and comes from the root word *'affuere,'* which means 'to flow to.'

In our roles as holistic life coaches so many people have told us they wished they had followed their joy and swum toward opportunities earlier. When asked what stopped them, they say they lacked the courage to follow their convictions and push through their fears.

Some feared making a mistake. Others only listened to the frightened, fearful part of their personality. They all listened to a voice that stopped them from reaching for their dreams.

Are you ready to reinvent your life and achieve your greatest potential? Or are you too comfortable—stagnating, not growing, nor challenging or exciting yourself?

Perhaps it's the fear of the unknown, or starting over, failing or succeeding. Fear is part of the human condition. It reminds you you're alive. It doesn't have to stop you from succeeding.

You must summon the courage to follow your destiny, whatever, wherever and with whoever it may be, with joy.

You only get one shot at life. Don't spend it regretting opportunities you never took and dreams you never lived.

Don't settle for okay. Live a significant, unskippable life.

How would your life be different if you were flowing toward, not away from, the fulfillment of your highest potential?

What would you do if you were 10 times bolder?

8

THE COMFORT RUT

"When we harness the forces of harmony, joy and love, we create
success and good fortune with effortless ease."
Deepak Chopra

It can feel easy sometimes to stay in bed, not challenge yourself, give up on joy and settle for less.

Sometimes people trade off their deeper joy for material comforts and status that can only ever give fleeting satisfaction. They get stuck in the comfort rut.

They settle for their actual self—what's easy, comfortable, familiar, or an area of competence in which they excel. They settle for a stagnant plateau that doesn't stretch or fulfill them or enable them to grow. Outwardly, they may appear happy and successful but in fact, they are bored, frustrated, and flat.

We all like to be comfortable, to do well and feel a sense of safety and security, but the comfort rut is a bit like staying in bed—we just keep lying around because it feels comfy and familiar. We may convince ourselves that we're happy in maintenance mode, but in our heart we know it's time to make the leap to an invigorating change.

Sometimes the signs of being in a rut are not obvious. But there may be warning signs—emotionally, mentally physically and spiritually—that we should heed. Do any of the following sound familiar?

- You don't feel inspired about your life or work
- You have trouble keeping your focus
- You feel tired, and find it hard to get motivated
- You reminisce about the past, or
- You worry about your future

Can you think of some comfort-busters you used in the past to pull you out of a rut in your career or life? What helped you recharge and find new inspiration? Perhaps it was a change in location; making new friends; rediscovering what intrigues you; revisiting your goals; taking on a new challenge or learning something new.

Sometimes the best way to gain a fresh perspective is to step away for a while. Take a long vacation or grab a short break, unplug from the world and enjoy some 'me' time. When you gain some distance from your life, everything looks clearer and summoning the courage for change is easier.

Making a leap into a new life and being true to your ideal self can be the most comfortable, joyful, liberating feeling of all.

How could any discomfort you may be feeling now benefit you if you push through?

What rut-busters would help support and invigorate you?

9

AUTHENTIC JOY

"Joy is the spark that fuels us to express who we really are. Never deny joy, for that is to deny who you are, who you truly want to be, and who you will be."
Cassandra Gaisford

You can't fake joy. Joy is your soul. Your essence. Your true self. Joy lives in your heart—not your head. You may not be able to define joy, but you'll know when it shows up.

Joy elevates.

Some people may try to talk you out of your joy. They may laugh at you, warn you, or even scold you.

Listen, but don't listen. It's fine to be open-minded. Less fine to be close-hearted. Some people may want you to follow their joy. They may want you to live the life they never lived. They may be acting out their fears and anxieties and trying to keep you safe.

Safe from what? The call of your own soul?

Oprah Winfrey once said, "I had no idea that being your authentic self could make me as rich as I've become. If I had, I'd have done it a lot earlier." On her climb to success many people told her to change her name. Gosh, it's hard to imagine a world without Oprah.

Of course, being authentic is more than a name. Many people live their authentic lives wearing the protective cloak of a pen name, nom de plume, or pseudonym. For example, Mary Ann Evans might never have found success as an English novelist in the 1800's if she hadn't written as George Elliot. Lady Gaga, has shared many times how her stage name empowers her.

Being authentic means having the courage to persevere despite fierce emotional storms. Had novelist Danielle Steel allowed jealously, envy and the dredging up of her private past by toxic media, to force her into the shadows of anonymity and shame, her ability to make a living from her authentic joy would have been thwarted.

"Envy is a very ugly thing and very dangerous. You have to protect yourself from it every day," Danielle Steele once said.

Who are you? Who or what do you yearn to be?

How could caring less what others think enable you to follow your joy?

JOY AT REST

"Peace is joy at rest. Joy is peace on its feet."
Anne Lamott

Our body talks and very often it's asking us to rest. But so many of are caught in the cult of busyness we ignore the warning chatter. When you've been a busy person for a long time it can be a real adjustment finding joy in resting when your body cries out for it. Rest requires coming to terms with stillness and all the thoughts that flood our minds.

"Work is the road to salvation", we are told. "Sloth is a deadly sin," we are reprimanded. "Do more and have more," we are encouraged.

Busyness can be a dangerous distraction though, and it's important that we learn to find joy in being still and being alone.

Meditation is a beautiful way of finding joy in resting. Being aware of your surroundings, being at peace with them, coming to a place of stillness within your mind, being mindful of the healing space that lies within are just some of the benefits that flow.

You don't have to close your eyes to meditate. All you need to do is just be. Be really conscious of how your area and environment look around you. Can you find ways to de-clutter and make a sanctuary to immerse yourself? Do you have old products that are ready to go?

Finding joy in resting can also come in the form of joyful journaling. Being aware of your thoughts as they bubble up to the surface and noticing any that no longer serve who you are and who you long to be and transforming them as they arise. Be mindful and notice which thoughts are negative and which ones are of a more positive nature.

Thoughts are energy and energy can be changed. With a little practice, patience, and perseverance we can lift our vibe higher. It's often the lower-vibe thoughts that we are trying to flee that capture us when we look for distractions.

Yes, it helps to have a purpose, but if we cannot stay still and find joy in the resting moments, then we have a problem. The call for joy asks us to please, please make time for rest.

How can you find peace in rest? What thoughts, feelings, behaviors need to change, and what needs to remain the same?

PUSH THROUGH

"Once you choose hope, anything is possible."
Christopher Reeve

Can you imagine how depressing it must have felt to have once played superman and then to become confined to a wheelchair for the rest of your life? Such a fate befell actor Christopher Reeve following a horse-riding accident.

Perhaps life has paralyzed you. Even though you might not feel like getting back up after a fall, it's important to push through. Feel the fear and play the game of life anyway.

Your power play may be pulling yourself out of your little rut and soaking up some sunshine. We truly do run off solar-batteries.

Here's what Hannah wrote before finishing this chapter:

I don't really feel like writing anything right now but I will because I am making a conscious choice to contribute towards this book. To push through my lack of inspiration and find inspiration where I am.

Mustang Sally is playing in the background of the cafe where I am and that's funny as it's actually my little theme song and I have chosen to find some joy in that.

It's not possible to feel joyful and inspired all the time but it's really about choice. Choosing how you want to feel and not falling prisoner to negative feelings.

I could've gone back to bed but I have decided to stick to my routine and come down to Prefab cafe and work on this book. Committing to some sense of routine and wonderment.

Joy at play is where the light shines through the cracks. This is where hope reaches us. Diving into dreams can be playful too. I dreamed that I went live inside my Facebook group and did a proper live video. It was really inspiring and soul serving. It was a sweet dream of showing up after a long period of hiding in the shadow.

"I can overcome anything from this space. I can be filled with wonder and enlightenment," Hannah says.

Anything can be achieved when we are filled with hope and wonder and joy. Who is the first person to achieve this? The internal, ideal you. The actual self, the lower version of ourselves might struggle, but then wakes up and realizes they she can, in fact, achieve anything and everything. The ideal, actualized self is liberated. You rise above your suffering and become a better version—your ideal self. You can find her from deep within, she is there. Forever and always. Invite her out to play.

Believe in your playful, inspired dreams. Dream them and bring them into being. Dream your new-found confidence into being. Don't compare yourself to others and measure where they are within their own growth process. You're not going in that direction. You're forging your own path.

When you show up, show joys up too. Feel the fear and play the game of life anyway.

What would it take for you to push through?
Who can encourage you to keep going?

12

GLORIOUS GRATITUDE

"I learned about the inextricable connection between joy and gratitude, and how things that I take for granted, like rest and play, are as vital to our health as nutrition and exercise."
Brené Brown

When you feel love, joy, gratitude, awe, curiosity, bliss, playfulness, ease, creativity, compassion, growth, or appreciation, you're in your beautiful mind.

Your beautiful mind is in a stream of transcendence and flow. Your spirit and your heart are aligned, and your best self comes alive. Nothing feels like a hassle, everything feels peaceful. You feel no fear or frustration. You're in harmony with your true essence.

YOUR SUFFERING MIND

When you're feeling stressed out, worried, frustrated, angry, anxious, depressed, irritable, overwhelmed, resentful, or fearful, your suffering mind has taken control.

Negative feelings and emotions—the uglies—become the norm, even if you'd prefer they weren't.

His Holiness the Dalai Lama reminds us, "Nothing beautiful in the end comes without a measure of some pain, some frustration, some suffering."

Reframe your uglies. Take back control, find and prioritize the beauties—the things that spark joy, that give you pleasure and bring deep satisfaction to your mind, body, and soul. Express gratitude for these and other things that are going well in your life.

These may be everyday things you take for granted, like kind friends, or being able to walk or a warm, or a comfy bed in which to rest. Or sensory delights, like the smell of fresh coffee, or freshly cut grass, or a whiff of your favorite perfume. Perhaps a stunning photo or a painting sparks joy, or a fabulous piece of architecture. Or, the vivid blue of a summer sky.

Look for the beauty within things you may associate with ugliness. Acknowledge any pain, frustration and suffering as a rite of passage and celebrate what's beautiful in your life to reclaim your joy.

When you're grateful for joy, joy spreads.

Wrap your day in gratitude.

Tell someone you're grateful they are in your life.

Compliment or thank a stranger who sparks joy.

STEP 2: DISCOVER YOUR JOY

The tips numbered **13-24** will help you to identify your own sources of joy and joy criteria. Answer the questions found on each page and complete the exercises suggested.

Try to be open-minded and consider all possible sources of joy. Be patient and maintain faith. Identifying your joy and purpose may not happen overnight, but it will happen if you allow yourself to dream a little and to notice the times you feel more joy.

Your sources of joy may be a complete surprise. It may be something you have not even considered before. Judge not what you feel joyful about—see only if it serves you and who you want to be.

When are the times you feel most energetic and fully alive? Who were you with? What were you doing? Did time seem to fly?

13

JOY'S CLUES

"Joy is energy. It is one of the highest vibrations on earth. Like love, it is impossible to define precisely, but easy to see and feel when it is present."
Cassandra Gaisford

How will you know if you have found your joy? Some common signs include:

- A feeling of limitless energy
- A feeling of deep peace, calm, and contentment
- A deep longing
- A feeling of inspiration
- A feeling of being surrounded by light
- A sense of excitement
- A state of arousal
- A clarity of vision
- A feeling of being empowered
- A sense of caring deeply

- A feeling of being connected to God, the Divine, Source energy
- A feeling of enduring happiness

What clues does joy give you? You may want to create a joy journal to capture the signs for future enjoyment—discover how in the next chapter.

KEEP A JOY JOURNAL

"I love quotations because it is a joy to find thoughts one might have, beautifully expressed with much authority by someone recognized wiser than oneself."
Marlene Dietrich

We've been keeping a visually-themed journal for years and so many things we've visualized and affirmed on the pages, are now our living realities. Houses, lovers, friends, health and careers—they've all been created on the page first.

Visualization is a powerful technique used by many successful business and sports people. See and record your way to joy.

If you spend time imagining the future you want, you have without even knowing it begun to make it happen.

Keep track of the times you notice clues to your joy. Record these moments in an inspirational journal so that they don't get lost or forgotten. This is where finding your joy and manifesting your preferred future really happens.

Adding quotes, articles, pictures, and insights from this book, anything that reinforces feelings of joy, passion, and purpose, will really make your journal come alive.

Gain greater awareness of what drives your joy by asking yourself, "Why does this spark joy?"

Look for the themes and patterns that build. up over time. Keep your joy alive by referring to it regularly and looking for more ways to add joy to your life.

When are you going to start creating your joy journal? What will be your opening image?

FOR SOME TIPS TO **help you create your own inspirational joy journal, watch Cassandra's television interview and interview with other experts here:**
http://www.cassandragaisford.com/media

IF YOU NEED MORE HELP to find and live your life purpose you may prefer to take Cassandra's online course, and watch inspirational and practical videos and other strategies to help you to fulfill your potential.

JUMPING WITH JOY

"Joy is the highest vibrational state we can experience. It feels light, uplifting, and exciting."
Hannah Joy

Joy has phenomenal energy and incredible versatility. In *The Book of Joy* the Dalai Lama shares that Paul Ekman, a longtime friend and famed emotions researcher, has written that joy is associated with feelings as varied as:

- Pleasure (of the five senses)
- Amusement (from a chuckle to a belly laugh)
- Contentment (a calmer kind of satisfaction)
- Excitement (in response to novelty or challenge)
- Relief (following upon another emotion, such as fear, anxiety, and even pleasure)
- Wonder (before something astonishing and admirable)
- Ecstasy or bliss (transporting us outside ourselves)

- Exultation (at having accomplished a difficult or daring task)
- Radiant pride (when our children earn a special honor)
- Elevation (from having witnessed an act of kindness, generosity, or compassion)
- Gratitude (the appreciation of a selfless act of which one is the beneficiary)

Buddhist scholar and former scientist Matthieu Ricard has added three other more exalted states of joy: rejoicing (in someone else's happiness, what Buddhists call mudita) delight or enchantment (a shining kind of contentment) spiritual radiance (a serene joy born from deep well-being and benevolence).

When you tap into your joy, you tap into an unlimited reservoir of energy and enthusiasm.

The French take it further—of course! *Jouissance*, literally means orgasmic joy. It's derived from the word *jouir* ("to enjoy"). *Jouissance* is to enjoy something a lot!

One of our favorite creativity experts Mihaly Czikszentmihaly, refers to this as a state of "flow."

In a popular YouTube talk he asks, "What makes a life worth living? Money cannot make us happy," he says. Instead, he urges us to learn from people who find pleasure and lasting satisfaction in activities that bring about this state of transcendent flow.

Coco Chanel was flowing when she designed her clothes, she was flowing when she attended to the minutest details of her garments. For her, her work had a spiritual aspect, it wasn't a job, it was her vocation and her deepest purpose—to liberate women from corsets and clothes that constricted their freedom.

Coco Chanel knew that you can succeed at almost anything if you follow your joy. This is where your soul meets the road—accelerating you toward your preferred future and fueling your success.

Find something that sparks joy and keep hugely interested in it by feeding and nurturing your *jouissance* every day.

Encourage yourself, challenge any mistaken assumptions and boost your belief by collecting examples of people who followed their joy and made a rewarding career or enriched their lives.

SOURCES OF JOY

**"Judge not about which you feel passionate. Simply notice it, then
see if it serves you, given who and what you wish to be."**
Neale Walsch

Joy goes in all directions. It can be as tangible as a job or car or a
house or as intangible as a dream or an idea. You could be joyful about
anything:

- A cause
- Analyzing things
- Books
- Magazines
- Sports
- Clothes
- Computers
- The future
- A belief
- A movie star

- An idea
- Astrology
- Saving the planet
- Your family
- Music
- Meditation
- Running your own business
- Crocheting
- Knitting
- Butterflies
- Joy!

Or something else.

What captures your interest and attention? List as many things as you can that you could be, or are, joyful, passionate, and purposeful about.

17

WHERE'S YOUR SUPERNOVA?

"Find out who you are—then go do that."
Dolly Parton

A supernova is a powerful and luminous stellar explosion. It's your point of brilliance—the areas in which your skills, talents, natural knacks and god-given gifts collide with your values, personality, dreams and deepest interests. It's where you truly shine.

People often ask, "How can I find out what I'm good at? What are my talents?" and "How can I be sure that I will enjoy it and succeed?" Sometimes, if their self-esteem is low, they'll say, "What's so good about me anyway?"

Whilst the answers may be evasive, the past is often a good predictor of the future. Often we just need reminding of the times and circumstances in our life when we felt inspired or energized by something, when our skills just seemed to flow, and of the outcomes, successes and positive feedback we achieved. These memories provide important clues to your joy-fueled talents, unique gifts and blissful brilliance.

Bliss is the home of our God-given talents. To activate their potential and reap the benefits we need to bring them out to play.

"The accompanying state of joy is quite distinct from the thrill of success; it is a joy of inner peace and oneness with all of life," writes David Hawkins in his fabulous book, *Power vs. Force: The Hidden Determinants of Human Behavior.*

Harnessing our supernova energy often requires a willingness to step outside our current comfort zone and challenge ourself to soar beyond what we think, or believe, we are capable of. Often it means leaving the safety of our areas of conscious competence.

"It is notable that this transcendence of the personal self and surrender to the very essence or spirit of life often occur at a point just beyond the apparent limit of the athlete's ability," says Hawkins.

"This phenomenon, is commonly described in terms of pushing oneself to the point where one suddenly breaks through a performance barrier and the activity then miraculously becomes effortless; the body then seems to move with grace and ease of its own accord, as though animated by some invisible force."

Cassandra experienced this when she embarked on her first attempt at writing a historical novel. Some of the early feedback she received included, "Sheer brilliance." No one was more surprised than Cassandra as she hadn't believed she could write such a book. She believed she didn't do 'detail' well enough to tempt such a massive project. But the subject fascinated her. The words and ideas just seemed to flow from somewhere beyond her.

Hannah felt animated by some invisible force when she 'came out of the spiritual closet' and offered her services as a spiritual conduit several years ago.

She feels joy when people tell her how she has helped them to connect to Spirit. Hannah knows how powerful and healing it is to be connected to Divine Energy.

Cassandra won an art award once, and her first attempt at an oil painting was selected as a finalist in a prestigious portraiture award. It seemed so effortless that she was completely thrown.

We don't say this to boast, but we wanted to share with you that in both cases, and many more, we always experienced self-doubt, and seldom possessed the confidence or belief that we had talent. But we did what made our soul sing, and challenged ourselves to show up, be who we are, do that, and share our work anyway.

Perhaps you may set yourself a similar 'stretch' goal, or you may be blissfully content to explore what energizes you and keep your talents hidden. Either way, it is in the act of following your bliss that you will find great joy and personal fulfillment.

Where is your supernova?

1 8

GET TO KNOW YOURSELF

"The great teachings unanimously emphasize that all the peace,
wisdom, and joy in the universe are already within us; we don't
have to gain, develop, or attain them. We merely need to open our
eyes and realize what is already here, who we really are."
Anon.

In his writings *Meditations*, The Roman Emperor Marcus Aurelius
demanded his readers know themselves and interrogate themselves
fully so that they could see their own capacities and limitations. Only
then, he suggested, could we achieve our greatest potential.

Within us we have the potential for brilliance, genius, magic.
Mining for gold enables us to bring forth this richness. Blending
emotion and reason keeps us from wandering too far into our own
fears, doubts or drifting off into fatal fantasies. Consult the list below
and discover ways to increase your self-awareness:

- Seeking and collecting feedback from others. "What is my
  superpower?" you may ask.

- Make a list of your favorite top five skills. Balance this with your blindspots or areas for development
- Listen to your body barometer for signs of bliss, flow, passion, love and joy
- Mine your astrological profile for insights
- Complete a skill or personality test

When we know ourselves we can realize our true value, discover our essence and access the field of pure potentiality to fulfill our destiny.

How could you get to know yourself better?

FOLLOW YOUR PASSION

"I spent decades leaning toward fear. But as I progressed on my spiritual path, I began to think, What would my life be like if I just leaned toward joy?"

Gabby Bernstein

As we shared at the beginning of this book, following your bliss is a great antidote to stressful striving. Whether we refer to the things, people and situations that fill us with happiness as sparking passion, joy, love or desire, these powerful heart-felt emotions are natural opiates for your mind, body and soul.

Charles Kovess, the author of *Passionate People Produce*, describes passion as: "A source of unlimited energy from the soul that enables people to achieve extraordinary results."

Often when you're feeling stressed, the things that you love to do are the first things to be traded. When you tap into something you deeply believe in and enjoy you may be amazed at the results.

Passionate joy brings the energy or chi of love, giving you energy, vitality and a heightened sense of well-being. It's one of the greatest stress-busters of all, and promotes the generation of endorphins—feel-good chemicals that will give you an extra spring in your step. Even five minutes a day doing something you love can give you your mojo back.

What may start off as a hobby could very well turn out to be your ticket to a more fulfilling career. Like for Brian Clifford, owner of Integrated Pest Management, who had always been fascinated with bugs.

After becoming disenchanted with his first career, he opted to follow his passion and became a "pestie." He loves the idea of being a white knight coming to peoples' rescue.

What do you love doing?
What inspires you?
What makes you feel joyful?
Identify these things and make some time to follow your bliss.

WHAT MAKES YOU ANGRY?

"You should be angry. You must not be bitter. Bitterness is like cancer. It eats upon the host. It doesn't do anything to the object of its displeasure. So use that anger. You write it. You paint it. You dance it. You march it. You vote it. You do everything about it. You talk it. Never stop talking it."
Maya Angelou

Bede Jarrett, once wrote, "The world continues to allow evil because it isn't angry enough."

Passionate anger, constructively used, could become the fuel that drives you, the fuel that drives your joy and purpose. The fuel that brings joy, happiness, peace and healing to the world

What presses your buttons? It may be specific things going on in your life now or wider issues about life in general, such as injustice, racism etc.

As we sit down to write this chapter Cassandra feels incensed by the apathy and incompetence in the mental health system. So much of it is guesswork masqueraded as professional mastery and science. She asked Hannah's medicating psychiatrist how the drugs she was prescribing worked and the doctor said, unblinking, no one knew.

"Fifty per cent work, and fifty per cent of the time it doesn't," she said. Yet she went on to tell Hannah that she would have to be medicated for the rest of her life.

No mention of holistic approaches, no mention of lifestyle changes, no mention of dietary changes that could help Hannah lead a healthy, empowered life. And the psychiatrist completely dismissed Cassandra's questions about alcohol-induced psychosis as being irrelevant. "This is unheard of in people of Hannah's age group," she said.

As a rule, Hannah doesn't drink alcohol, and only drank moderately over many years. However, like many people, when stress flared, alcohol called.

While the mental health system is a big beast to turn, Cassandra channels her 'anger' into her writing and self-empowerment books to help bring to light 'truths' people may not know. She repays a debt of gratitude to novelist Danielle Steel who shared the tragic account of the battle her bi-polar son had and his subsequent loss of life.

Are there any ways you could you use your anger to benefit others and bring about positive change?

Gain greater awareness by exploring why your buttons are being pushed.

21

WHO INSPIRES YOU?

"The very essence of diamonds
is to bring joy into the lives of people."
William Goldberg

Who or what inspires you? Think about the sorts of books and maga-zines you love to read, or people and things you love to listen to, learn about, follow or be around. What about them is interesting to you? How do they bring joy into your life?

Look for your heroes and heroines and allow others' enthusiasm and passion to excite you! Play detective. Do some research, go and talk to people who are joyful and purposeful about some aspect of their life, read books about inspiring people or themes that really capture your imagination. Listen to podcasts, watch Youtube, and other uplifting sources of inspiration.

As Cassandra writes this chapter, she's inspired by the 2020 US Presidential candidate Marianne Williamson. She loves the values she espouses. She loves her tenacity and eloquence. She loves her inclusiveness and willingness to use her voice to create positive change. She loves her powerful spiritual manifesto.

She has inspired Cassandra to become more active in her community to reduce alcohol harm. Marianne has inspired her to begin planning her three billboards to increase awareness of safe alcohol consumption leading up to, and during, the Christmas season. At such times drinking spikes and so does domestic violence, sexual assault, drink driving deaths, suicides and other forms of harm.

At the time of writing Cassandra met with the police, her local MP and the Mayor and spoke to a major booze retailer to gain support and build awareness of her initiative. She was encouraged when the policeman in charge of reducing alcohol harm said: "I'm really looking forward to seeing your billboards."

Cassandra was inspired by the movie *Three Billboards Outside Ebbing, Missouri* about a mother who was frustrated nothing was being done to find her daughter and so she created billboards to build awareness of her plight. And also her friend Christine who said, "Gosh that billboard woman reminded me of you."

Cassandra saw the movie three years or so ago. Now she has finally become passionately inspired enough to do something about it. She's not talking campaigning to make everyone teetotal, she's found purpose in spreading more awareness of safer drinking.

Because nothing was being done by the government who only seem to talk, talk, talk. Cassandra decided to do something herself. As she writes in *Mind Your Drink: The Joy of Sobriety*, the booze barons and litigious lobbyists currently yield more political and economic power than those whose lives they destroy.

Cassandra gives thanks and gratitude to presidential candidate Marianne Williamson for her activism and encouraging us all to be the change we want to see and reminding us that we as a people can wield power.

What could you do to get more inspired? How can you, too, become a source of inspiration for others?

22

BE YOUR VALUES

"What we seek with deep longing, here and there, outside and beyond; we find at last within ourselves and we give to others with joy."
Cassandra Gaisford

What do you care deeply about? What are your deepest beliefs?

Your values are your deep, personal needs, and the things that are truly important to you. They represent who you are, who you want to be and what you want to contribute to the world.

You may have a deep need to be creative, to help others, to entertain people or to change the world. Anything.

When your values are met there can be an incredible sense of joy, but value conflicts can also be a powerful clue to your joy and purpose.

Discovering all the things that you feel strongly about is not always easy. Look for some clues to your beliefs by catching the times you use words such as 'should' or 'must.' Or, even the times you find yourself saying or feeling that you really 'want to' do something.

What do you really believe in? It might be honesty, openness, freedom, equality, justice, compassion, generosity, kindness—or something else.

Real joy is more than a fad or fleeting enthusiasm. It can't be turned on and off like a light switch. It's a full-bodied belief or commitment to something.

Choosing and then acting like the person you want to be is your own personal code of honor. It's the founding statement of behavior you set for yourself. It's your commitment to yourself.

What are your values? Or what values do you now choose to embrace? Below are a few to consider:

- Freedom
- Peace
- Joy
- Helping others
- Autonomy
- Activism
- Love
- Calm
- Optimism
- Loyalty
- Creativity
- Compassion
- Being empowered

Identify and acknowledge your values.

How can you be your values?

What do you need to experience, feel, or be doing to feel deeply fulfilled?

Record your insights in your joy journal.

23

GIVE JOY

"If you want joy, give joy to others."
Deepak Chopra

Prior to writing this chapter, Cassandra felt 'compelled' to donate a second painting to the local hospice who were holding an art auction to raise much needed funds.

She felt a surge of joy as she drove along the country roads of The Bay of Islands and headed toward the township of Kerikeri with her painting, 'Blossom' in the backseat. She felt delighted when the Fundraising and Awareness Manager, for Hospice Mid-Northland greeted *Blossom*, "Wow. That's brilliant," she said. "Thank you so much. I love it."

"Everyone needs cheering up at moments like these," Cassandra said, referencing the fact that the people they care for are dying. "I hope it brings a few moments of happiness and joy. I know how healing creativity can be."

Cassandra shared with her the memory of her step-father Ted, a military man, who in the final stages of brain cancer, began to paint watercolors. Brilliant watercolors they were too—surprising everyone who had known him.

Painting brought Ted a few precious moments of joy and peace, and escape. And when he left this world, we had them framed and they were the gift that kept on giving.

"Love. Joy, Prosperity. Hope," Cassandra said, reading out the words she had painted in French, to the Fundraising and Awareness Manager.

It is the intention behind your giving and receiving that is the most important thing. The act of giving, doesn't always have to involve giving something away for free, but it should always be joyful. It should always be to create happiness for both the giver and the receiver—then the energy behind the giving multiplies, spreading seeds of joy among the world.

What can you gift or do to give joy to others? It doesn't have to be a physical thing, it may be by volunteering, dressing joyfully, sending a kind thought or a prayer, or the willingness to forgive.

Go do that:)

24

FIND AND FOLLOW YOUR PURPOSE

"Your purpose is to live your joy."
Marilyn Harper

If you want to create more joy in your life finding and following your purpose is a good place to invest time and energy.

However, this is an area where many people struggle. The US Center for Disease Control recently reported that 40% of Americans have not discovered a satisfying life purpose, and lack any idea of what makes their lives purposeful and meaningful.

It is well known that having purpose and meaning in your life increases not only life satisfaction but also promotes mental and physical health.

Many successful authors, for example, testify to the power of writing with purpose and sharing their stories and purpose-driven words.

So, where and how do you find your life purpose? "The wound is where the light comes in", said the Persian poet and mystic Rumi. Many people have found their life purpose following their recovery from trauma or adversity of some kind. For Hannah and Cassandra, this is the catalyst for this book.

"It is in giving that I connect with others, with the world and with the divine", says author Isabel Allende. Following the death of her daughter, who fell into a coma in 1991 and never recovered, she poured her grief onto the page and wrote a memoir as a tribute to Paula's life. She still receives letters from people who tell her how much her book, *Paula*, helped them through their own grief.

Self-help icon Louise Hay's personal philosophy was forged from her tormented upbringing. Her childhood was unstable and impoverished, and her teen years were marked by abuse. Louise started what would become her life's work in New York City in 1970.

Hay attended meetings at the Church of Religious Science and began training in the ministerial program. She became a popular speaker at the church and soon found herself counseling clients. This work quickly blossomed into a full-time career.

After several years, Louise compiled a reference guide detailing the mental causes of physical ailments and developed positive thought patterns for reversing illness and creating health. This compilation was the basis for *Heal Your Body* which is also known affectionately as "The Little Blue Book."

Cassandra forged a successful career helping people find their passion and purpose following negative work experiences which robbed her self-esteem and threatened her health and vitality.

Our purpose? To encourage and inspire others and help people live and work with beauty and joy.

Your life purpose may not evolve from the transcendence of your own wounds, but it's incredibly fulfilling when your life purpose empowers others.

What gives your life meaning and purpose?

STEP 3: JOY AT WORK

Tips 25-36 in this section will help you to identify and explore work options and ways to develop your career in light of your joy and purpose.

You'll be asked to consider what your beliefs are about the role of joy in your career and the workplace. Is finding a job you love a realistic expectation? What role do you think joy should and can play in your work life?

Exercises in this section will also help you isolate your joy criteria for job satisfaction. What do you need, and what do you wish to contribute, to feel purposeful about your work?

The tips in this section will help you generate lots of possible career alternatives and to decide on your best-fit career options. Ask yourself why you consider these your best choices. Do they meet your joy criteria? What are some of the steps you need to take in order to make these options a reality?

25

JOB FULFILMENT

"Whatever life gives you, you can respond with joy. Joy is the
happiness that does not depend on what happens. It is the grateful
response to the opportunity that life offers in this moment."
Brother Steindl-Rast

We spend too much time at work to give up on joy and purpose, but
some people think that you save the things you love for a hobby or for
when you retire.

The truth is you are unlikely to find real fulfillment or meaning in
your work unless it engages you as a person and delivers some kind of
buzz.

Joy-filled employees are good for business too. People who love
their work are productive, happy, engaged and inspired.

If you can't find joy in salaried employment, embrace a side hustle,
volunteer elsewhere or spark excitement by considering the freedom
and fulfillment of being your own boss.

Numerous people have found tremendous joy in the most unexpected places and very often it has been born from a place of great
pain.

Here are just a few examples of people who are living and working with joy:

- New Zealand Prime Minister Jacinda Ardern
- Novelists Danielle Steel, Isabel Allende and many others
- Drew Barrymore, especially in her new business, Flower Beauty
- Trauma Therapist Dr Edith Eger
- Neuroscientist Dr. Joe Dispenza
- Motivational author Gabby Bernstein
- Comedian Billy Connelly

What role could joy play in your working life?

26

WHAT LIGHTS YOU UP?

"There is no mistaking love. You feel it in your heart. It is the
common fibre of life."
Elizabeth Kubler-Ross

If you want to feel happy in your job you need to be clear about all the
things that lights you up and make you feel passionate and alive.

Let's say we work 40 hours a week in a job we absolutely love.
Doing something we love causes the release of the happy 'feel good'
hormones, dopamine, serotonin, and oxytocin—often called the 'love
hormone.'

Endorphins, our body's natural pain reliever, also increase when
we engage in reward-producing activities that spark joy.

Ensure a natural high. Using what you've learned from the
previous pages, make a checklist of your joy factors for job satisfaction. Some things to consider include:

- Your values, beliefs, and deepest interests
- Your strengths and skills you love using

- The sort of work environment that suits you best
- The people you want to work with
- The things that fill you with purpose
- The skills you'd like to develop
- Your personality and what makes you tick
- Your income needs or aspirations
- Your health and lifestyle needs

Numerous studies have found evidence that doing what we love and following our soul's calling is the Swiss Army knife of all things healing.

YOU'LL FIND MORE suggestions to help you ensure you make the right career decision toward the end of this book in the section, Your Point of Brilliance. Plus we'll affirm the importance of not overworking and taking extremely good self-care.

Create a 'What Lights Me Up' checklist and list or summarize your non-negotiable joy factors.

Refer to your list when making any career decisions.

27

AUTHENTIC HAPPINESS

**"When I wrote I didn't think of the time
or the problems, all I saw was the joy and passion of it."**
Annie Featherston

As Annie Featherston, writing as Sophia James, shares in Cassandra's series *Mid-Life Career Rescue,* when you combine your favorite skills with doing something you completely and utterly love, you come home to your true Self and find your place of bliss. The result? Contentment—and a scalable career.

"I'd taught for fifteen years and loved it. And then I didn't.

It wasn't the students or the workload. It wasn't the noise or the constant worry of, 'was I doing enough' that pushed me out either.

I was a good teacher but underneath was a passion that I couldn't ignore any longer. I wanted to be a writer, a historical romance writer, and I was beginning to get offered some wonderful opportunities that did not meld with the structured teaching year and the constant pressure of it.

I felt like a juggler with a hundred balls in the air. I was teaching part-time, taking tours to Europe with my husband to help him, running mentorship programs…. and writing.

Writing was my complete and utter love and yet it was always taking a secondary place. I wrote at night. I wrote in the weekends. I wrote when the kids were asleep. When I wrote I didn't think of the time or the problems, all I saw was the joy and passion of it. I loved forming characters and thinking of stories. I lay in bed at night asking my protagonists questions and spent many hours trawling over history books to place them into a context.

I have a degree in history so it was as if all the things I had enjoyed were coming together at last. History and writing. I knew that at 54 I couldn't be patient any longer.

I needed to be in a field that I felt fully aware in, that I loved beyond the weekly paycheck and that filled my spirit with lightness.

I'd just won a New Zealand based competition for a completed romance and it was validation, I suppose. If I didn't make the jump and do it now perhaps I never would. And if I never gave myself a chance I would feel bereft.

I penned my resignation letter and left to Australia to be a mentor on a five-day intensive scheme the Romance Writers of Australia were running. It was scary and hard but when I finished it successfully I remember standing alone in front of the mirror, a cold sore from exhaustion and worry on my lip, but my clenched fist punching the air in triumph.

To feel like that is to know you live.

When I got picked up by Harlequin Historical and published it felt like all the dreams I had hoped for so long were finally happening. I had visualized this. I had walked the lonely windy beaches of Gisborne and shouted my hopes for it into the wind. I had sat in the mall with three crying children in the car and written scenarios on the back of the supermarket docket because the story just wouldn't wait until I got home.

If I had not been paid one cent for my writing I would still have done it somehow. But the strange thing is that money does follow passion and suddenly I was making as much as I ever did in part-time teaching.

Writing is hard work. A book does not come fully formed from thin air or dreams for me. But I've persevered and sat and written. I've made deadlines. I've written blogs. I have delved into social media and stood there with a smile on my face when the reviews have not been what I wanted.

But I have always believed in myself and my stories. I've kept going. I have never given up.

And I have loved my writing life, my freedom, the creativity, the possibilities.

If I had my time over I would have left my teaching career earlier. I would have been braver and less worried by all the sensible advice others were giving me. I should have listened to my heart and taken the jump into a lifestyle that is my perfect fit and even if I had never succeeded I would have known that at least I tried."

We love Annie's story of reinvention. So-called sensible advice is no replacement for the wisdom of your heart, your soul, your intuitive knowing about what choices are right for you.

What frightens (or empowers) you more—the fear of change or the fear of not changing? What's the best thing that could happen if you made a change for the better?

What are your favorite skills? Which skills and talents come most easily or naturally to you? Which ones give you a buzz or a huge sense of personal satisfaction?

How could they combine with an area of interest or enthusiasm to create a new calling or career?

BE OBSESSED

"All my life I've wanted to do something big."
Burt Munro

New Zealand motorcycling legend Burt Munro proved that obsession is the key to success. "All my life I've wanted to do something big," he said. In 1967 Burt achieved something huge.

At the age of 68, against all the odds, he set a world record of 183.586 mph with his highly modified Indian Scout motorcycle. To qualify he made a one-way run of 190.07 mph, the fastest ever officially recorded speed on an Indian.

Like so many inspiring people the road to success was not an easy one—it involved much personal hardship and numerous setbacks, but armed with his passion and a compelling desire to "go out with a bang," Burt Munro mortgaged his house and set out on the greatest adventure of his life.

His truly awesome achievements were bought to life in an inspiring and uplifting film, *The World's Fastest Indian.*

The World's Fastest Indian not only gives movie-goers an inside look at Munro's passion, but it also gives them an idea of New Zealand filmmaker Roger Donaldson's overwhelming desire to tell the story.

"This project has been a passion of mine since I completed a documentary about Burt Munro back in 1972," Donaldson said. "I have been intrigued by Burt's story for many, many years; some would say my obsession with this film matches Burt's obsession with his bike."

A HEALTHY OBSESSION can lead you to many things, including your:

1) Life niche—creating a breath of fresh air and giving you a competitive edge

2) True bliss—leading you to your vocation where being paid is the icing on the cake

3) Your point of excellence—unleashing dormant talents and natural gifts

4) Your life purpose—spreading seeds of joy and inspiration and benefiting others.

When does time seem to fly? When was the last time you felt really excited, or deeply absorbed in, or obsessed by something? What were you doing? Who were you with? What clues did you notice?

How could your obsession create an overwhelming desire careerwise?

WE'LL EXPAND MORE on the importance of knowing the difference and health implications of healthy joy versus overjoy in Step 4.

DREAM YOUR DESTINY

"You must learn to follow your destiny, whatever it might be, with joy."
Paulo Coelho

You may like to think of destiny as a destination—a career path you would like to follow. It sounds easy, but often the hardest part is figuring out what you truly want.

Get closer to your destiny and generate joyful career options by letting your imagination run freely. The following exercise will help unearth your buried desires:

Imagine you've just been cloned. You are now five people! Each of you has gone in a completely different career direction. There are no constraints—money is not an issue. You can get any job you want and you're getting all the experience you need.

What would each person be doing or willing to try? Isolate and list the key elements that make each of the five careers you identified satisfying to each clone.

Carol a disillusioned counselor whose role was made redundant, wanted to get away from always hearing about people's problems. She came to Cassandra for coaching as she was finding it hard to identify roles which would excite her.

Before coaching, she wrote, "I'm starting to question whether I'm doing the right thing applying for jobs at the moment. It's stressful and I'm afraid I may end up in a role that I don't want. I'm feeling quite conflicted at the moment."

Cassandra thought the cloning exercise would be a great way to stimulate her sense of possibility and remind her of the things that gave her joy. Joy, one of our other clients reminded us recently, is the fruit of your spirit.

At first, Carol was skeptical. It all sounded very impractical. Cassandra encouraged her to let go of her rational mind and play with possibilities. Once they had a few ideas down, she reassured Carol that she could look at 'concrete' career options then.

Her clones included: being a financially successful global coach; a non-fiction writer; an artist traveling the world; a creative educator; and the creator of a thriving community.

Together they isolated all the elements that made these roles fulfilling to each clone and stretched the boundaries further by exploring how these clones could combine into what Cassandra calls a 'career combo'—a combination of careers strengthened by a core theme and united under one rainbow.

"I'm feeling excited," Carol said, as together we set about planning how she could make her career combo a reality.

IF YOU IDENTIFIED a role that combines many jobs or have just invented a new job title, begin to think about where you could find a market or outlet for it. It may be that you do a 'career combo'—a little bit of this and a little bit of that!

Clone yourself. Look for the themes.

How could you turn your dream into a reality?
What are all the possible options?

3 0

JOB SCULPTING

"Imagination is more important than any other trait for my work
and such an easy skill to develop. Never look where you think you
should, the creation of a new idea is simply combining two or
more existing concepts together. A new idea can be either
unfamiliar, silly or both."
Mark Olsen

If you are already employed, but not really enjoying it, try the
following exercise. It's about identifying your needs and then taking
steps to have them met.

'Job sculpting' is a technique from the Harvard Business School
that involves tapping into the psychology of work satisfaction and
matching people to jobs that allow their interests to be expressed.

Analyze your current job description or job function and isolate
the areas you enjoy most and enjoy least. If you are out of work, you
may find it helpful to consider what you liked and didn't like in
previous roles.

Now start sculpting by identifying ways you could chip away at the tasks that don't fulfill you and actively adding on the tasks and responsibilities that you are passionate about.

Develop a strategy to make the changes you desire a reality.

By sculpting your dream role, you stop being just a passive reactor and start being a co-creator in your life.

How could you tailor your current role to increase the amount of time spent on activities that make you happy?

If you are unemployed, how could you use the skills and experiences from your previous role to create your best-fit career?

THINK LATERALLY

**"The man who has no imagination
has no wings."**
Muhammad Ali

Brainstorm and list as many possible career options as you can that would allow you to work with joy and fulfill your joy and purpose. Think laterally and don't close down too many ideas.

Have you considered self-employment? How could you tap into economic, demographic and social changes to create a product or service that really excites you and for which there may be a future demand?

When Elizabeth Barbalich founded her successful company *Antipodes* she tuned into the growing interest in New Zealand products and natural skin care, free of animal testing.

What do you feel called to do? Hannah felt called to heed the call of spirit and to help others tune into their divine wisdom too.

The aim is not to make a decision at this stage but to build an exhaustive list. Make it fun. If you run out of ideas ask friends, family, and others to contribute ideas. Check out websites such as www.ca-reers.govt.nz for job ideas.

Are there any ways to earn an income from your joy and purpose that you haven't thought of or which don't exist yet?

What economic, social, and cultural changes could lead to a future opportunity for you?

How could you fulfill a need?

32

COLLABORATE TO SUCCEED

"There are souls in this world who have the gift of finding joy everywhere."
Jean Paul Richter

Collaboration happens when two or more people or organizations work together to complete a task or achieve a goal. At its finest it works within the spirit of cooperation—coming together for mutual inspiration and benefit.

Don't be afraid or too proud to ask for helping hands, hearts and minds. 80% of all jobs are never advertised in newspapers and job-search sites. Lots of opportunities go unnoticed and some are created when you knock on the door.

Don't let someone else steal your thunder.

Keeping an ear to the ground and using personal contacts is the key to success. It's not just what you know, but the people you know or could get to know!

Network with other like-minded people. Talk to other joyful job seekers, check helpful websites, and network with organizations that provide tips and examples to help you succeed and stay positive.

Ask your way to success by identifying and proactively networking with everyone who can help you achieve your goal. You don't have to go it alone. Even Sir Edmund Hilary didn't climb Mount Everest by himself!

Draw up a list of organizations or industries where you'd love to work. If your joy is helping others, identify all the organizations whose core mission is to help. It sounds simple, but you'd be amazed how many people never think to begin their job search by looking at areas of shared interest and enthusiasm.

If the idea of self-employment rings your bell, collaborating for success will prove to be a winning strategy. Learn from those who have pursued this path and succeeded.

GET CAREER-FIT

Make sure you are prepared for the new, joyful you! Update your resume ensuring it's tailored to match the opportunities you're pursuing. Brush up on your interview techniques.

Many people feel uncomfortable promoting themselves. If this is you identify strategies that will help you through the self-marketing phase. Remember that you serve nobody by keeping your light under a bushel.

Who could you collaborate and connect with for mutual benefit?

What three things can you do to get career-ready?

YOU'LL FIND PRACTICAL, inspiring and empowering tips and strategies in Cassandra's *Mid-Life Career Rescue series.*

33

THE NEW WORLD OF WORK

"If you don't have a way of raking in extra cash, it's probably because you haven't figured out your side-hustle yet."
Alana Massey

Work doesn't have to be a 9 to 5 drudge. Change your relationship to work. If you can't do the thing you love full-time you may be able to do it part-time.

Many people today work on a project basis or do several, different jobs instead of having just one vocation or career. Some people combine salaried work with self-employment or a hustle on the side. Others do it because they're looking for fulfillment outside their nine-to-five job.

Your side-hustle could be a once-a-year gig or something you do in your spare time (hello, Uber and Airbnb.) Whatever the mode and motive, side-hustling is the new world of work.

Working more flexibly could help you to get more variety, stability, joy and purpose into your life. It's also a great way to update or flex your skills, explore new interests, and prepare for your next career move.

What do you want to get out of a side hustle?

How could you repackage your working week?

3 4

ANALYZE YOUR OPTIONS

"We cannot solve our problems with the same thinking we used
when we created them."
Albert Einstein

Once you have generated a reasonable list, decide on your best career
options. Start analyzing which ones are most achievable for you. How
well do they meet your joy criteria and life goals?

Avoid dismissing your ideas prematurely or acting impulsively. It's
a good idea to use a variety of thinking styles to assess suitability and
fit. For example ask questions such as:

- What are the facts?
- How do I feel?
- What works? (i.e. strengths and positives)
- What's possible?
- What could go wrong?
- What's the next step I need to take?

QUESTION YOUR ASSUMPTIONS

Don't buy into the myth that feeling joyful about your work is a dream obtainable by only a few. Reality test your own beliefs or fears.

Look for examples of people who are earning an income from pursuing their joy and purpose.

Interview for information and inspiration by talking to people already working in areas they are passionate about, or those who are doing the job you want.

Who could you talk to?

What "facts" do you need to check out?

How could you test your reality further?

35

TAKE YOURSELF ON

"We know that when we *feel* a feeling of love, compassion, understanding, forgiveness, we change our self-esteem. There is an effect that changes the electrical and magnetic fields in our heart and that those fields literally change the stuff that our world is made of."
Gregg Braden

Life isn't all rainbows and sunshine, magic and manifestation. Shit happens. Life can suck. We can feel stuck. To flourish, the reality is that despite what is going on around us we have to spark feelings of joy, love, and peace. It's not always easy. It can seem impossible. Sometimes we have to accept that we are an orchid in the desert, a triangle in a hexagonal hole.

Staying stuck in a job that doesn't match your vibration or your goals and makes you feel resentful, hateful, or downright depressed will never deliver the energy elixir you desire. We need to make a concious choice to keep our vibrations high while we plan our great escape, leap into our essence, and make a career change for our highest potential.

Imagine if Duff McKagan (former Guns n Roses legendary guitarist) had settled for being a pastry chef instead of pursuing his dream to be a rockstar. What if author Isabel Allende had settled for being an outspoken and censored journalist instead of chasing her literary dreams?

Imagine if J.K Rowling had remained in an abusive relationship instead of accepting help from social security, remaining on a benefit and using the time to write the books she held in her heart.

None of these things would be possible if Duff, Isabel, and J.K. hadn't taken themselves on. Our dreams, our fears, our circumstances, and perhaps even our laziness—and all the other life circumstances that hurl themselves in our way—test our self-esteem. We are asked to question how much our dreams really matter.

Love doesn't always show up on time. The road to victory is not always a straight line. Many people have a hard time believing that money will easily come to us if we do what we love. Staying in a job we hate just for the money may be a good short-term decision, but in the course of a few years, we're likely to suffer. If we stay in a job we loathe, we're taking out a high-interest loan on our health.

If you really want to feel joy at work and live a life with purpose you have to desire it more than you'd believe. You have to fight it, you have to fight yourself. It's not easy. Keep going. Don't quit before the miracle happens.

How can you marinate yourself and your dreams in love, compassion, understanding and forgiveness?

How can you keep going?

36

BOOST YOUR SELF BELIEF

"You've got to believe in what you're doing. You can't stay in the void of self-doubt. It's holding you back. It's like a bike—you've got to let go of the training wheels and say, "I can do this. I can do this without the training wheels."
Laurie Wills

Does the quote above say something to you? It did to Cassandra when her partner gave her a motivational blast, back in March (2015).

Her previous lack of confidence surprised so many people who knew her. She'd always adopted the 'fake it 'till you make it' policy when needed. But self-doubt had always held her back from tackling some of the bigger projects she yearned to do.

"You can't make a living from something you love," a woman said recently. We hear that all the time. You might have too. Or, maybe deep down, there's a persistent voice telling you, you're not good enough, or you can't have what you want.

But what if the opposite were true? What if making a living from what you love is exactly what you can do.

It's the messages you tell yourself that matter most, says celebrity Hypnotherapist and Author Marisa Peer. "Belief without talent will get you further than talent with no belief. If you have the two you will be unstoppable."

Chances are you don't need to see a therapist to move beyond self-limiting beliefs, but if you do, great. Go do it. We have. There's magic in that.

You can also learn from some of the most powerful, effective and simple techniques used by practitioners working in the realm of positive psychology and mind reprogramming.

"When our strategies are simple and solution-oriented, we can develop effective and compelling futures," says the founder of Solution-Focused Brief Therapy, Inso Kim Berg.

The questions below, drawn both from Solution-Focused techniques, and Cognitive Behavioral Therapy (CBT), could help you challenge your fears and move forward courageously.

ACTION QUESTIONS: CHALLENGE YOUR BELIEFS

Acknowledge the things you don't believe and challenge them. Interview your beliefs, by asking them the following questions.

"Where's your evidence for that?" (That being whatever you fear or hold to be true?)

"What's the worse that could happen if you pursued your joy? How bad would that really be? How can you increase the likelihood of success?"

"What tells you that you could follow your dreams?" (This is a nice shift from focusing on the problem to looking for solutions instead.)

"What have you tried recently that worked? What are you doing now that works?"

"Who do you know who is happy at work? What could you learn from them?"

"How does your (supportive other) know you can do this? What difference will it make to them when you are happier?"

Believe it! When you let desire, not fear propel you forward, magic happens. It's the Law of Attraction. The Law of Manifestation. The Law of Intention. But it only works if you stay positive. Negativity is a repellent. Positivity is a magnet, drawing abundance forward.

SHIFTING INGRAINED BELIEFS

So often we aren't even aware of what our self-limiting beliefs are. If your beliefs are ingrained, or you keep sabotaging your own success, seeking help from a qualified practitioner with expertise in repro-gramming stubborn, disempowering beliefs may be a game-changer.

Believe in what you do and who you are and the gifts you have to offer. Allow no doubt.

STEP 4: LIVE YOUR JOY!

We have to try and live and work in the joy zone as much as possible. It sounds simple, but most people don't.

Why don't more people live their joy and purpose? Reasons vary and are numerous, some common ones include:

- Lack of Balance
- Overwork
- Stress
- Exhaustion
- Distraction
- Trauma, wounds, and illness
- Being caught in the comfort-rut
- Fear
- Toxic thinking
- Negative addictions
- Low self-esteem
- Lack of confidence and self-belief
- Being in the wrong environment

TIPS NUMBERED 37-55 in this section look at ways to help you inject more joy and purpose into your life. You'll also discover how to overcome obstacles to joy, from stress and anxiety to trauma and illness, and how you might be able to experience joy even in the face of these inevitable challenges.

We'll look at joy beyond the world of work and the issue of achieving work/life balance.

You'll be asked to consider some possible barriers to joy. And you'll be encouraged to consider any psychological issues that may need to be worked on so that you can fulfill your potential.

Where are you now and what do you want? What could stop you from doing the things you are joyful about? How could you live a more passionate and joy-filled life?

This section will suggest strategies to maximize your success and overcome obstacles. How can you take greater responsibility for living a more joyful purposeful life? What will you need to do? What will you need to change?

3 7

HEALTHY HOBBIES

"A hobby a day keeps the doldrums away."
Phyllis McGinley

"An idle mind is the devil's playground," some people preach. One way to get out of overthinking or overworking and to jump into your joy and purpose is to help yourself to a hobby.

Joy can come from throwing yourself into something new and creating new habits. The neural pathways in your brain will forge new connections and fuel a happy high as you engage in something purely for pleasure.

There are a plethora of different hobbies to choose from. You might like to try something musical, or artistic like painting or sculpting, or creative like cooking, dancing, crochet or knitting. Perhaps something with more vigor may tick the boxes, like mountain biking, hiking, or martial arts.

Super sensitives like we are, often operate out of our higher minds in the spiritual realms. As a result we need good grounding hobbies. These include gardening, yoga and meditation.

You might not feel joy when embarking on a new hobby. When Hannah took up crochet she felt overwhelmed at first. Your chosen interest may stretch you beyond your comfort zone. You might find when beginning something new that some unwanted emotions surface.

Don't be thwarted. Let them come to pass. Embrace a beginners mind and adopt a child-like curiosity to see what may unfold. This may be a latent gift or talent, or a dormant interest, or some fun new friends.

For Hannah, crochet lead to unexpected feeling of joy. The joy of discovering something new. The joy of mastering a new craft. The joy of thinking, worrying, and fretting less.

The truest definition of a hobby is something you do in your free-time purely for pleasure. So, by definition, its something that you do to connect to your joy.

Whether your joy is something you do with others or a joy you experience on your own, the benefits are the same. According to a Western Australian study, even just engaging in a hobby for two hours a week can dramatically improve your mental and emotional health.

Cassandra knows from her own experience, that as little as 15 minutes per day spent on things that interest her, sends her joy levels soaring.

The gift is the ability to take your mind away from stressful striving or feeling in the doldrums and into something personally pleasurable.

Side-step the cult of busyness. Remember to make time for hobbies—because they're fun, make you happy or enable you to truly recharge.

Having an outlet for your interests and somewhere to channel your feelings is really important in your quest to recover joy or to maintain better balance in your life.

What hobby could you resurrect? Is there something you would be interested in trying just for enjoyment?

38

UNLEASH YOUR INNER CHILD

"A moment of joy can erase months of uncertainty and sorrow for a Human who is desperate to see the light of laughter."
Kyron

Joy is the staple of children, who seek it out, demand it, and use it to its fullest. Their natural state is laughter. The energy of the Inner Child belongs to us all.

Laughter, humor, and play are great tonics during stressful times. Taking yourself or your life too seriously only increases stress. When you learn to laugh despite your difficulties, you light up the world—for yourself and others.

"When people just look at your face," the Dalai Lama said to the Archbishop Desmond Tutu in *The Book of Joy*, "you are always laughing, always joyful. This is a very positive message. It is much better when there is not too much seriousness. Laughter, joking is much better. Then we can be completely relaxed."

Laughter triggers the release of endorphins, your brain's feel-good chemicals, setting off an emotional reaction which makes you feel better.

"Discovering more joy does not, I'm sorry to say, save us from the inevitability of hardship and heartbreak. In fact, we may cry more easily, but we will laugh more easily, too," says Archbishop Tutu.

"Perhaps we are just more alive. Yet as we discover more joy, we can face suffering in a way that ennobles rather than embitters. We have hardship without becoming hard. We have heartbreak without being broken."

You may not feel like it, but give laughter a go. Watch a funny movie, stream a stack of whacky comedies, go to a comedy show, or watch a video on YouTube. Hang out with people who know how to have a good time, go to a Laughing Yoga class, or ask someone to tickle you!

Inject some more laughter and playfulness into your life.

Playfulness is bounciness at its best. Cultivate your inner child. Act up a little, goof-off, experiment, relax and detach—if you find yourself in trouble, smile.

Benefits of play include:

• Increasing your productivity
• Boosting your creativity and problem-solving skills
• Reducing stress, anxiety, and depression
• Improving your relationships and connections with others
• Bringing more balance, fun, lightness, and levity into your life
• Diminishing your worries

As play researcher and psychiatrist Stuart Brown says in his book *Play: How it Shapes the Brain, Opens the Imagination, and Invigorates the Soul*, "A lack of play should be treated like malnutrition: it's a health risk to your body and mind."

The Dalai Lama agrees. "I met some scientists in Japan, and they explained that wholehearted laughter—not artificial laughter—is very good for your heart and your health in general."

Some of the many ways Cassandra plays include: 'wagging' work sometimes and taking her inner child on a playdate to the movies, going for a massage, or indulging in her hobbies and playing with her paints. While traveling internationally recently, she watched the Disney children's movie *Frozen*. She hadn't laughed so much in years.

For Hannah listening to music or singing is playful and brings levity. She also loves hanging out with her good friends.

"I can't express the joy I have with my amigos here," agrees Dr. Bruce Lipton.

Author Deepak Chopra confirms the power of lightening up, "When we harness the forces of harmony, joy, and love, we create success and good fortune with effortless ease," Chopra says.

How can you unleash your inner child? Who or what brings out your playful side?

39

OVERJOY

"Perhaps there could be no joy on this planet without an equal weight of pain to balance it out on some unknown scale."
Stephenie Meyer

Joy is fab, but too much of something good can be bad, bad, bad. When we are filled with purpose and fun, throwing ourselves into something we love with such a passion we can't get enough, can quickly and easily lead to burnout.

Hannah recently learnt this lesson a brutally hard way. It's important to find balance even when you really enjoy something. This is where we bring it back to the critical importance of self-care.

Making sure you have your daily rituals and practices to ground you and keep you centered is crucial. This is especially true when your joy is of a spiritual or ungrounded nature.

Working as a spiritual entrepreneur Hannah loved the work she did so much she totally overdid it. When we overwork, poor choices, including lack of sleep and a low-vibe diet can follow.

Hannah is finding her way back to joy by changing her work

model. Less time on social media. Making sure she instills clear boundaries by not being available all the time. And making space for hobbies and downtime. These are some of the many strategies she has employed to regain and sustain her mental health and life balance.

When we are passionate about our work and value helping others, we can sometimes give too much. We have to learn to give to ourselves and this can be difficult. But not as difficult as completely frying out.

Another form of overjoy, can be Toxic Positivity—a preference to avoid the expression of negative emotions, like anger. Suppressing any emotion ultimately traps it in our bodies and can manifest later as disease. Again balance is key.

Valeria Teles, a personal trainer and author, says she was shocked to realize that her obsession with physical fitness had taken over her life.

"In working with clients, it became clear to me that they were forcibly engaging in exercise for reasons other than to supplement their already happy lives and "fit hearts." They—and I—were using exercise as a form of escape from a reality rooted in the fear of illness and death, in emotional pain, and in the struggle to find happiness and peace," Valeria says.

In the following chapter we share some of our daily self care rituals that nourish our days and nights.

How can you find more balance in your life?

What do you need to do less of or more of?

What are you daily self-care practices?

40

MAGIC DAILY ROUTINES

"Getting into my body, even for 30 seconds, has a dramatic effect on my mood and quiets mental chatter."
Tim Ferriss

"If you win the morning, you win the day," says millionaire author, podcaster and polymath Tim Ferriss. Despite his phenomenal success Tim suffers from anxiety and credits a robust morning routine and other health behaviors with giving him more joy.

Like Ferriss, we kick-start our day with 10-20 minutes of transcendental meditation, five to 10 minutes of journaling or Morning Pages, making our bed, and a healthy dose of positive vibes. We also engage in some light exercise—a nice brisk walk or some gentle yoga.

Below are just a few of the many *Magic Morning* routines and rituals you can use to prime your day for miracles:

• **M**editation and mindfulness—enjoy some sacred silence
• **A**ffirmations—empower your beliefs with feeling-based reminders of your intentions

• Goals to go for—set your priorities, including health and well-being activities (exercise, etc.)
• Inspiration—journaling, visualization, reading
• Co-create—partner with spirit, tap into your Higher Self, evoke the muse...and get ready to create

Importantly, complete these crucial focusing activities *before* you get to work or jump into your day.

Pushed for time? We experience many of these activities simultaneously when we meditate, write our Morning Pages, and consult the oracles; and also when we go for a walk in nature, listen to an uplifting audiobook or podcast, or sip our morning coffee.

Recently, to help improve our quality of sleep we've created a Nice Nights Routine:

• Nourish your mind—mindfulness, meditation, affirmations, or enjoying some sacred silence
• Inspiration—journaling or affirming gratitudes, visualization
• Celebrate—acknowledging achievements and successes
• End the day—setting intentions for the following day, including health and well-being goals, partnering with Spirit (prayer, evoke the muse...) and entering our dreams

Take the time to reconnect with your higher self, and elevate your joy, resilience and happiness levels.

Get your day off to a high-vibration start. Choose, develop, and apply your own Magic Morning routines.

Seal the day with your own Nice Evening shutdown.

41

STRESS LESS. SENSE MORE

"Rejoice in the pleasures of being a personality in a sensual
physical body, occupying a world that provides enjoyment
alongside the hardships we face."
Sarah Varcas

If stress, anxiety, or depression has stolen your joy, looking for things
that nurture you and sanctify and awaken your senses can be a great
tonic.

Surrounded yourself with things that spark joy. For example,
incense or essential oils for smell; crystals around you for sight;
Hearing wonderful flute music and Arabian and Oriental tunes for
sound; Drinking freshly squeezed fruit, if you find it hard to stomach
much else. For touch, you may love to draw in a mindfulness coloring
book or book a massage.

Regularly ground yourself with meditations, journaling your
thoughts and feelings and being in your own safe, sacred, snuggly
sanctuary.

Limit the things that trigger stress, like over-work, email, social media and stressful communications on your phone.

One of Cassandra's favorite go-to strategies is aromatherapy. "Nature works holistically...and so do we," says Clinical Aromatherapist, Andrea Butje.

The simple truth is that even if you are unaware of the power of smell, aroma affects your mood—and those around you. Best of all, this joy booster, doesn't require you to do much at all—just select a yummy essential oil, smell and inhale. If your joy could do with support, the following blends can help enhance peace, happiness, delight or rapture:

BLEND #1
- 3 drops Bergamot
- 1 drop Ylang Ylang
- 1 drop Grapefruit

BLEND #2
- 1 drop Geranium
- 2 drops Frankincense
- 2 drops Orange

ANOTHER FAVORITE STRESS-BUSTING strategy we both enjoy is regular massage. If lack of sleep is robbing your joy, you'll be pleased to know that a one hour massage has the same health benefits as six-hours sleep. Plus you'll be ridding yourself of joy-draining toxins.

Investigate the power of smell. What scents imbue you with happiness, joy, and well-being?

If stress is taking a toll you'll find more comprehensive, easy to apply help in, *Stress Less.Love Life More.*

JOYFUL MEDITATION

"Mediation keeps me sane."
Stella McCartney

Our brains never get a break and the results can be increased stress, anxiety, insomnia and if left unchecked, depression, psychosis and mental crisis.

But there is something you can do—meditate. You may know this already. Perhaps you're already a convert. Or you may be like us—sometimes we're so busy being busy that we forget to prioritize time for joyful meditation.

It helps to remind yourself of the many, many benefits.

According to Psychology Today, meditation is the strongest mental practice that has the power to reset your happiness set point, thus turning you into a more joyful person and literally rewiring major areas in your brain.

Meditation changes brain patterns, soothes a frazzled mind, and connects you to your Higher Self. "It's the Swiss army knife of medical tools, for conditions both small and large," writes Arianna Huffington, the founder of *The Huffington Post* and author of *Thrive*.

So, what's the buzz? Recent research published in *New Scientist* has revealed that regular meditation can tame the amygdala, an area of the brain which is the hub of fear memory.

People who meditate regularly are less likely to be shocked, flustered, surprised, or as angry as other people, and have a greater stress tolerance threshold as a result.

By meditating regularly, the brain is reoriented from a stressful fight-or-flight response to one of acceptance, a shift that increases contentment, enthusiasm, and feelings of happiness and joy. Here are a few of the many ways a regular meditative practice will help you bounce with joy:

- Decreased stress and anxiety
- Improved focus, memory, and learning ability
- Heightened recharging capacity
- Higher IQ and more efficient brain functioning
- Increased blood circulation and reduced hyperactivity in the brain, slower wavelengths and decreased beta waves (Beta State:13—30Hz) means more time between thoughts which leads to more skillful decision making
- Increased Theta State (4—8Hz) and Delta States (1—3 Hz) which deepens awareness and strengthens intuition, visualization skills and mysticism
- Increased creativity and connection with your higher intelligence

There are a wide range of ways to meditate. Cassandra practices transcendental meditation. Hannah prefers a form of guided mindfulness.

It took Cassandra a while to get into meditation—her friends thought it would be impossible to sit still and turn off her, then, over-active mind. But since she discovered that the majority of world-class performers meditated, she decided to make it a joyful habit.

Her practice of meditating for 20 minutes in the morning and 20 minutes at the end of the day yields remarkable benefits.

Perhaps you're afraid of quiet. Afraid of what you might hear or find when you come face-to-brain with your mind. If you're afraid of silence it may pay to find a way to befriend your higher self and acknowledge the benefits of some quiet time alone. Still, no one says a little company will do you wrong. Whatever works for you, right?

For those wanting some help getting started apps like *Headspace*, *Calm*, or *Breathe* are great. Or take a class or go on a retreat.

Regularly take time to focus on the present moment. Make meditating for at least 20 minutes a day part of your daily routine for optimum success and well-being.

What's your go-be-quiet strategy?

43

ONE LOVE

"What's the one thing I can do that will make everything easier?"
Gary Keller

We live in an era of noise and distraction. Mindlessly scrolling through our social media accounts; multitasking between 15 different topics; watching TV while reading a book and texting a friend and taking a selfie—or something else distracting.

Our energy becomes displaced, frenetic, chaotic. Neurons fire haphazardly in our brains—left, right, up, down, vertical, and diagonal all at the same time. We're like the Pinball Wizard, with everything lit up and all the bells ringing—and we're playing on 50 machines.

Our laptops and computers have 20 tabs open, mirroring our minds. We live in an era of chaotic disarray. Making it even more important to slow down, seek some moments of quiet, and focus on one love.

"Engaging in subjects of too great a variety confuses the mind," Leonardo Da Vinci once said. Instead, settle down quietly and ask your Higher Self, "What's my one thing, which if I did it everything would be better?"

Finding space for your one thing often requires moments of quiet. Quiet can include meditation, yoga, looking at an object for a set period of time, watching clouds fly by. For some people quiet is found scuba diving or immersed in a flotation chamber where they can just be.

As Cassandra writes this chapter she's aware of all the unfinished projects she has yet to complete. Like many creatives she finds joy in variety and likes to multitask. But sometimes she overwhelms herself with all she has yet to finish. During such times her greatest strength becomes her greatest weakness.

She has to bring the balance back in moments of quiet and center again and gain clarity about what is most important to her. She reminds herself to bring her attention back to one love—the writing or task she is doing in this very moment.

It's easy to become distracted by the false sense of achievement as you knock off easy tasks. It's easy to crave the dopamine spike enabled by the sense of completion when you tick things off and closing down a tab—or five.

It's often the little things which, like flies, buzz annoyingly and demand our attention. But tackling a significant project, an extraordinary pursuit, the challenge of going beyond our own expectations, setting a very high goal—one that will be difficult to achieve—truly sparks joy.

There's magic in going beyond one's limits. And it's in these moments of quiet that we are reminded of this.

How can you make space for quiet and find and finish your one thing?

44

WHAT'S YOUR STORY?

"Owning our story can be hard but not nearly as difficult as
spending our lives running from it. Embracing our vulnerabilities
is risky but not nearly as dangerous as giving up on love and
belonging and joy—the experiences that make us the most
vulnerable."
Brené Brown

Whatever may be holding you back, creating a new narrative begins
with dreaming your new existence into being. Create from within
yourself. Who do you want to be? Who do you not want to be?

If you're struggling to answer these questions it helps to think
about people who inspire you. Who has overcome the same obstacles
as you and where are they now? Can you look at their story and how
they changed to become the person that they are today?

For example Oprah Winfrey has always inspired us as she over-
came so much adversity to reach the place she is in now. She inspires
millions by sharing the trauma and the pain that happened to her and
putting herself in a vulnerable place.

Importantly, she shares that we do not have to become imprisoned by our old stories, we can be the heroes and heroines in our own lives. As Oprah has shown, we can create inspiring new chapters in our lives.

Fake it till you make it is such a powerful phrase. It might feel overwhelming, you might feel blank, the inspiration may not come, but if you connect to your guides and your source of internal inspiration, little buds will start to blossom.

Dreaming yourself into being begins with one short burst of inspiration and joy.

Create a script for yourself of who you want to be and write yourself your future reality then record it as a meditation to listen to to manifest your future into being.

Your new life vision doesn't have to be fixed yet, may be it's just a draft from which to build.

45

TRAVEL WITH YOUR TRAUMA

"I want our young people to know that they matter, that they belong. So don't be afraid. You hear me, young people? Don't be afraid. Be focused. Be determined. Be hopeful. Be empowered. Empower yourself with a good education. Then get out there and use that education to build a country worthy of your boundless promise. Lead by example with hope; never fear."
Michelle Obama

We live in traumatic times, by traveling with our traumas we can navigate our way to understanding ourselves and other people a little better.

We have a choice when it comes to taming trauma. We can run from it and let it defeat us or we can embrace it and allow it to become something better. We can delve deep into psychological awareness and educate and empower ourselves by understanding what's happening for ourselves and others.

You can use that education to extend compassion, sympathy, and understanding and journey into the mind of someone who is going through something you have suffered and survived yourself.

Trauma comes to us for a reason and a purpose. It comes to teach us more about ourselves, about our resilience and our capabilities beyond the trauma itself. We are so much stronger than we give ourselves credit. It's seeing past the fog to the strength beyond that illuminates the way through these traumatic times.

We have a choice. We can choose to let these things overwhelm us or we can fight back and be more positive for it. We can see the silver lining around any circumstance and choose positivity.

Finding joy in trauma is no easy task but with daily well-being practices like meditation, journaling, creative expression, essential oils, and other health behaviors, including counseling, you can find yourself returning back to your usual self.

The other side of trauma is connection and hope. When you heal yourself, you shine a light for others to follow in your steps.

How can you travel with your trauma and lead by example?

If you got out there and used your experience and education to build a country liberated from trauma, how would that feel?

How would it feel to help people thrive? Do that!

46

HEALING SORROW

"It was such a depressing time. I didn't look very depressed maybe but it was really dire. I made a conscious decision not to stop, but it could have gone the other way."

Dame Zaha Mohammad Hadid

Did you know you can die of a broken heart? Science has validated what we know to be true. Takotsubo cardiomyopathy, also known as broken-heart syndrome, occurs almost exclusively in women, medical researchers say.

Harvard Medical School reports that the condition is caused by a weakening of the left ventricle, often as a result of emotional or physical stress—such as the loss of a loved one or a sudden illness.

When things we love or value end we can feel as though life itself has died. We can feel depressed, despondent, stuck in a wasteland of 'nothing matters anymore'.

Life is a never-ending series of beginnings and endings. Life has its births and deaths. We have full moons and no moons. An ending is not a failure, but an opportunity for a new, and often better, beginning.

It's okay and healthy to 'keep it real' and allow yourself to feel low. If your boyfriend cheats on you or tells you he no longer feels 'the love,' or friends abandon you, how could you possibly feel happy? It's normal, and healthy, to feel sorrow. It's okay not to succumb to toxic positivity and think that life is only about having 'good vibes' and feeling continually inspired.

When painful things happen in our lives, this adversity may temporarily dull our joy, but remember that joy is energy. Like the sun, it will rise again and charge and enliven our lives.

Sometimes, hanging onto the light during periods of darkness means cutting yourself some slack and cultivating serenity. "God, grant me the serenity to accept the things I cannot change, courage to change the things I can, and wisdom to know the difference," the Serenity Prayer encourages.

Ultimately, surviving life's ups and downs involves being in touch with our Higher Power (God, The Divine, The Universe—whatever we believe in).

If we can practice radical acceptance, cede control, and hang onto the spirit of hope, every ending does bring a new and happier beginning. As sure as day follows night and spring follows winter, we can, *and will*, experience the joy of new and healthier jobs, minds, bodies, and relationships—even if it's just a better relationship with ourselves.

How can you mend your heart and heal any sorrow in your life? What worked in the past? What do you need to let go of? What do you need to hang onto?

What would it feel like, and what would it take to strengthen your connection to a Higher Power, cultivate courage and wisdom, and nurture the possibility of a fresh start?

47

JOYFUL SOBRIETY

"I'm very serious about no alcohol, no drugs. Life is too beautiful."
Jim Carrey

Many people mistakenly believe drinking alcohol will increase their happiness. Very often people self-medicate with booze (and other drugs), rather than seek alternative ways to heal their sadness or boost joy. But alcohol is a depressant and in large quantities is draining on your body and mind.

It's also a well-documented neurotoxin—a toxic substance that inhibits, damages, and destroys the tissues of your nervous system. Taken to extremes alcohol can even induce psychosis.

Increasing numbers of people are embracing the joy of sobriety by limiting their drinking or consciously deciding not to touch a drop.

"Not drinking makes me a lot happier," says supermodel Naomi Campbell.

Author and spiritual guru Deepak Chopra also gave up drinking. "I liked it too much," he once said. Steven King, after almost losing his family and destroying his writing career, managed to quit. Other people like Amy Winehouse devastatingly never made it. At only 27, she died of alcohol poisoning in 2011.

Risking destroying your career, ruining your relationships, sacrificing your sanity, and in the extreme, taking your life, is a massive price to pay for a mistaken belief that to be happy, or to numb your anxiety or cope with stress you need to drink more booze.

Our aim is not to preach, but to encourage you to explore your relationship to drink and approaching it more mindfully. You may wish to ride the wave of the sober-curious and consider, a period of sobriety. Instead of focusing on what you may be giving up, turn your mind to what you may gain—a better, more energized version of yourself.

The many benefits of reducing your alcohol intake, or not drinking at all, include:

✓ A stronger ability to focus on your goals and dreams
✓ Improved confidence and self-esteem
✓ Increased productivity
✓ Increased memory, mental performance, and decision-making
✓ Better control of your emotions
✓ Sweeter relationships
✓ Greater intuition and spiritual intelligence
✓ Authentic happiness

Not everyone battles with booze. Whether you cut back or eliminate alcohol entirely, the choice is ultimately yours. Only you know the benefits alcohol delivers or the joy it destroys.

Experiment with a period of joyful sobriety.

IF YOU NEED tips to help you moderate your drinking, *Mind Your Drink: The Surprising Joy of Sobriety*, available as a paperback and eBook will help.

48

FIT FOR JOY

**"We can recover from even the worst of trauma and pain and
become vital, joyful successful and flourishing again."**
Marky Stein

In her biographical, empowerment book, *Fit for Joy: The Healing Power
of Being You,* Valeria Teles poses a great question, "How do we exercise
a healthy and joyful heart, despite a painful past?"

So many of us run from our pain, we numb our shame, we seek
distraction in a myriad of addictions. But what if, instead of running,
we turned and faced our painful pasts, wrapped our loving arms
around our hurts, and chose to see the gift of the lessons we have
learned?

We only have to look to the great minds and hearts of Holocaust
survivor like Viktor Frankl and Edith Eger, sexual assault thrivers like
Oprah Winfrey, Maya Angelou, Billy Connelly, and Lady Gaga, and
'ordinary' men and women around us, who instead of becoming
victims or victimizing others, chose to use their pain to benefit the
lives of others.

As one of Cassandra's favorite authors Isabel Allende once wrote, "Without my unhappy childhood, what would I have to write about?"

We can become fit for joy. We can transcend the pain of our past, but like any fitness goal, it takes work. This 'work' may take the form of weekly therapy (some helpful ones for trauma include EFT, and EMDR). Some people prefer to seek spiritual counsel, others transcend their pain through various creative routes (painting, songwriting, singing, acting, dancing etc.). Others go down the self-help route. There is no magic cure, no one-size-flatters-all when it comes to transcending our hurtful pasts. But it is universally agreed, our wounds need to see the light.

"Suffer now, reap the rewards later,"Akshay Nanavati, Marine Corps Veteran, speaker, adventurer and author of *Fearvana*, reminds us.

When we make a commitment to our healing we become fit for joy.

What, if anything, is blocking or limiting your capacity for joy?

What what it take and what could you commit to in order to be fit for joy?

49

FEARVANA

"Fear is just excitement without breath."
Anon

At times it seems we live in a world marinated in fear. We often spend more time thinking of ways we could fail, fall, and fumble rather than ways we could succeed, soar and shine.

What if we embraced the joy of fear? What if nirvana lay on the other side of fear.

Focus is everything. As former US President Barak Obama once said, "I try not to focus on my fumbles—only on my next plan."

The hardest lessons and biggest fumbles often yield the ripest rewards. By being kind to ourselves we give ourselves and others permission to make mistakes, grow and learn.

Some people don't pursue their potential because they're afraid of success. Success can bring unwanted attention, criticism and the risk of failing.

Success can also be threatening to others who haven't achieved their potential—even your best friends can become your worst critics.

Unless we attempt to do something beyond our comfort zone we cannot learn and grow.

People often put more energy into resisting change and preserving the status quo than they do in embracing change. We can hold onto old stories, drag out old dreams, or cling to seemingly safer shores. When a door which once opened wide, slams shut we can keep pounding on rather than walk, heart wide open, in search of new joy.

Why is that?

Changing can be hard work. It means taking a risk and stepping into the unknown. Some people fear change because they believe they may lose what they have—even though what they have may be sucking their soul.

For many people change means taking responsibility and ending years of blaming others, being a victim, or living in denial or in a state of apathy.

What's worse—the fear of a few setbacks, or the disappointment of dreams never chased and potential left unfulfilled?

Allow yourself to feel the excitement of achieving the 'impossible' and surprising yourself!

Are you afraid of standing out? Are you prepared to be a tall poppy even though others may seek to cut you down?

How could your success inspire others? By feeling the fear and going for it anyway, how could you inspire yourself?

Look for and collect examples of people who have turned fear into joyful success.

50

KEEP YOUR THOUGHTS HIGH

"Thoughts carry a vibration. They can pull you down or lift you higher."
Cassandra Gaisford

For some people being in the vibration of joy may feel, initially, like "losing control" but actually it's a place where, instead of being controlled by the negativity of the mind, your being is in full control.

Joy is a high vibrational state of being. If your body has become accustomed to being predominantly in the lower vibrational states, it's bound to feel uncomfortable staying in joy for long —ironic as it might seem.

Your mind may struggle and find it uneasy to stay in a state of higher vibration—it can produce feelings of guilt, discomfort, insecurity and general uneasiness about orienting with the vibration of joy on a consistent basis, and may even want to cling to lower vibrational states—despite your wish to move to higher ground.

Attitude is everything. Be a guard for your words, thoughts, and feelings. Don't let self-doubt or poisonous thinking be the thing that deflates your joy.

Doubts and fears can be true, but they can also lie. They can keep you safe but they can also catastrophize. They can tell you nothing will get better. *Ever.* Not in a trillion and three years.

Refuting irrational, unhelpful or self-sabotaging thoughts is a key technique of Cognitive Behavioral Therapy (CBT). To free yourself of shackles that enslave, what if all you have to do is write or say a counter-sentence that could also be true?

<u>Unhealthy thought</u>: "I have lost my joy."

<u>Healthy thought</u>: "I will get my joy back."

Add some feeling words for greater power. For example, "I will get my joy back and it will feel amazing."

Be your biggest fan and self-soothe Back yourself 100%. We all have doubts, but it's amazing how your doubts will disappear once you are kinder to yourself and are doing the things you love.

Since fear and love cannot exist together—chose joy.

How can you cast toxic thoughts out and keep your thoughts high?

51

LET GO OF THE GUILT

**"Filling your own needs is not something
that you do randomly, it's something that needs
to be done on a regular basis."**
Cassandra Gaisford

Joy requires us to focus on our own joys and pleasures, rather than follow what everyone else wants us to be or do.

Many people don't follow their joy because they feel guilty for wanting more from their lives. They may have low or narrow expectations of what they should be getting out of life. Or they may feel an overwhelming sense of duty to others and they put everything and everyone else first.

You may be told that your being selfish. Or you may rationalize your situation with statements like: "Why can't I just settle? What's wrong with just getting by?"

Imagine how feeling happier and joyful could change your life and benefit others.

As you've read in Healthy Hobbies, you don't have to monetize your joy. There is health and healing in doing something you love, just because you love it or it gives your life purpose. There is pleasure to be found in private joys, just as there is in public joy.

Whether financial gain is the ultimate pursuit, or simply wanting to feel more peace and bliss, make following your joy a regular event.

If finding the time or lacking energy is preventing you from doing more of the things that fulfill you, develop a strategy to restore the balance.

Only 15 or 30 minutes a day devoted to activities that spark joy can make a big difference to your health and happiness.

Are you feeling guilty? Give up the guilt and prioritize your needs. Why shouldn't you put yourself first?

Can you do something every day to help keep your joy refreshed, loved, and alive?

52

LIVING IN THE JOY ZONE

"For me a home should transmit the joy of life."
Rosita Missioni

Sometimes to fertilize your joy a change in environment is a wonder cure. It may mean moving house, moving city—even moving country.

Cassandra escaped the city five years ago and found joy in the stillness and silence of the country.

The other day she and her partner were looking at a beautiful native tree which had self-seeded in a stream. Lorenzo said, "there's no life there."

They both knew that it would never reach its full potential bogged down in the swamp. To flourish it needed to be true to its nature and place its roots firmly in the soil.

Similarly, butterflies need to be out of the wind and in the sun in order to fly. They are often found at rest until the need to mate or seek food causes them to fly.

Cats are similar. they spend a majority of the time sleeping and then with restored vigor chase their intended conquest.

Some people are in their environment when they're surrounded by lots of noise and the hectic pace and hustle and bustle of a city or dead-line-drama-driven career.

For others this sends their central nervous system splintering. They need the quiet serenity of the country or some other sacred space.

Sometimes, all that is needed to shift into the vibration of joy is to find sacredness in your bed. 2020 US Presidential candidate Marianne Williamson says she pens some of her best ideas when she retires to her bedroom.

Where is your energizing environment? What do you need in order to be at one with your true nature and do your greatest work?

53

WHAT CAN YOU DO?

"It's a circle—the more you know, the more you remember. It's a circle. So yes, it gets easier, it gets better, it becomes more joyful."
Neale Walsche

When you're feeling stressed, depressed, forlorn or lonely it can feel is though it's impossible to summon the energy to do anything you love. But it is possible. It's possible to do a little thing. A small thing. A tiny thing.

Whether it's just taking one deep breath. Taking five extra steps. Or signing up for a class you're curious about and just sitting there absorbing the creative energy.

Hannah did this recently when she learned to crochet. One stitch at a time, she slowly felt her joy return. And as she waited, a new joy was created. A beautiful, happy hobby.

During low times in Cassandra's life she loves to sit in places of sacred silence. This may be the beach, the forest or the sanctuary of her bedroom. When she returned to Wellington to support Hannah after her release from hospital recently she decided to spark joy by going with her daughter to the healing harmony of Saint Mary's of The Angels. We lit a candle, said a prayer, and sat in sacred silence.

Then we went as planned to our health appointment and said what we needed to say and listened to what we need to hear.

We closed our ears to toxicity, negativity, and fear and opened our hearts to love, light, and learning. Learning how to grow. Learning how to flow. Learning, again how to listen to the wisdom of divine intelligence that resides within.

As above, so below, we were reminded. Spirit soars in heaven and on earth.

With one foot in front of the other we keep moving forward.

What can you do?

How can you remind yourself that whatever you are going through will pass and the sun will come again?

MAKE A JOY ACTION PLAN

**"To accomplish great things,
we must not only act but also dream;
not only believe but also plan."**
Antole France

Some people think that fate will take care of their future. But the winners in life know that failing to plan is planning to fail.

Written goals, with action points and time frames, are essential if you really want to achieve a more joyful life.

What, if anything, is stopping you from pursuing your joy? Really analyze what holds you back and develop a strategy to overcome any obstacles that may stand in the way.

REFLECT back on the strategies and tools you've discovered in this book. Complete the following exercise to create your plan of joy.

Personal Action Plan for Creating Joy

COMPLETE THE FOLLOWING:

I SHALL STOP DOING:

I SHALL DO LESS:

I SHALL DO MORE:

I SHALL START TO DO:

Make a joy action plan. Do something every day to help move you closer to your goal of leading a more passionate, purposeful life.

Don't forget to tick off and celebrate your achievements along the way to reinforce feelings of success.

How to Find Your Joy and Purpose is also available as an audiobook for your listening enjoyment. Check out a free sample or grab your copy from your favorite online retailer.

EXTRA SUPPORT: COMPANION WORKBOOK

How to Find Your Joy and Purpose (the book) offers you information about overcoming adversity, building resilience and finding joy. Reading a book is great but applying the teachings and writing things down in a dedicated space helps bring the learning alive, deepens your self awareness, and enables you to make real world change. Reading gives you knowledge, but reflecting upon and applying that knowledge creates true empowerment.

By writing and recording your responses you're rewriting the story of your life. As Seth Godin states, "Here's the thing: The book that will most change your life is the book you write. The act of writing things down, of justifying your actions, of being cogent and clear, and forthright—that's how you change."

The *How to Find Your Joy and Purpose Companion Workbook* will support you through the learning and show you how to create real and meaningful change in your life...simply and joyfully.

WELCOME TO THE JOY ZONE!

"If you don't shoot for your dreams, your dreams die with you, but the joy of trying lives eternal."
Hannah Joy

You've made it! By reading and applying the practical strategies in this book you've taken the first step to leading a happier and more fulfilled life.

You've heard the call, you know what brings you joy, contentment and bliss. You've found your capabilities, your aspirations, your long-ings, and your hidden talents. You've found your purpose and you know what makes you happy.

You now have all you need to embark on new experiences and to make life-affirming choices. You have all the seeds to plant new beginnings. You may feel a knot in your gut as you prepare to make a leap, but you're excited.

Your possibilities are infinite. You are empowered and in complete control of your life. Have a foot in the future but stay grounded in the present. Have faith and trust in yourself and your abilities. Plant the seeds of your aspirations, nurture and protect them, and watch them grow into the prosperous fruits of your passion.

Take a leap of faith and venture forth. Work and live with joy and purpose!

Well done! But remember, staying in the joy zone is a choice and requires an ongoing commitment. Like a fragile rose it takes time and effort and attention. But remember how great it feels when you're living your joy.

Keep this book handy and refer to it regularly. It will help you achieve your goals and keep your joy and purpose alive.

You've completed a tremendous and joyful journey. Thank you for allowing us to travel with you.

IN GRATITUDE AND WITH LOVE,

CASSANDRA AND HANNAH Joy

P.S. Before we part company you may find it helpful to summarize all that you have learned by clarifying your point of brilliance.

YOUR POINT OF BRILLIANCE

Your point of brilliance is where you truly shine. It's your point of joy and passion. It's the intersection of your favorite gifts, and talents, your deepest interests and enthusiasms, and all that motivates, inspires and drives you. It's the place of fire and alchemy, magnetizing and attracting people, situations and opportunities to you.

But you must show up and then your brilliance shines too. You must commit to being authentically you. And you must stand in your own truth. You know what makes you bloom and what makes you wither. You know when you're opening and when you're closing.

Be deliberate and focused in the pursuit of your happiness. Target your intentions on your dreams and desires, and ensure your choices align with what makes you happy.

Get real about your motives. Why do you want to reach your goals? Are your following your path with heart, your life purpose, your true destiny? If you follow your chosen path, will you reach your place of true bliss and authentic happiness?

Are you grounded in your truth, or are you chasing someone else's goals, or the lure of fantasy and ego?Remember the perfect career and life for you is one that:

- Fills you with joy and purpose
- You're passionate about
- Interests you
- Aligns with your highest values
- Utilizes your favorite talents
- Allows you to express yourself
- Fulfills your potential
- Facilitates your growth
- Feeds your mind, body and soul
- Boosts self-esteem and confidence
- Makes you happy
- Fuels your energy
- Gives life
- Enables your goals
- Completes your life
- Supplements your lifestyle
- Is your point of brilliance

These are not unrealistic expectations. Target your intentions, and shoot straight for the stars. Don't settle for anything less.

AFTERWORD

"You are cut off from Being as long as your mind takes up all your attention."
Eckhart Tolle

In writing this book we realized the importance of pressing pause —and we hope you have too.

In today's Always-On culture, it often feels like we spend every minute in motion—juggling unrelenting deadlines, balancing family demands, attending meetings, keeping up with social media, and more, more, more.

Get off the treadmill. Make a plan to find your joy and really discover who you really are and what you really want.

If you've reached a point where you need some thinking space; if you're so stressed or exhausted, or you feel completely overwhelmed; if you feel you've lost any connection with who you are or what you want s and crave a quiet moment, prioritize your needs. Take a sabbatical.

Plan some time away. Pick a time that's easier than others. A few weeks when taking time out won't be too disruptive.

Plan it to perfection. Do your handovers, put everything in place to ensure that things work smoothly in your absence, tidy up loose strands and importantly, make it clear you won't be contactable.

Plan not to do too much. Pick a place where you can decompress. Something that feels like a bit of a treat or a vacation. A retreat, where you immerse yourself in almost total silence may tick the boxes. Somewhere that couldn't be further removed from your normal life.

The change in pace may be challenging at first. You may find it difficult to switch off and stop. Your adrenaline may be running so high that you'll need to remind yourself of the need to calm down. Or you may be so used to multitasking and nurturing others that you need to learn how to put yourself and your self-care first.

Check-in with yourself. Take time to stop and allow yourself the space you need to think about your future self. Take time to do things more slowly. When you give yourself space and time in your head to feel calm, to slow down, reflect and make some big decisions you'll make wise choices. It's amazing what can happen when you invest in yourself.

Take the lead and pass it on. Tell everyone they should take a sabbatical and when friends tell you they feel inspired to do the same, tell them to stop thinking about it and just do it.

Don't wait to stage some kind of intervention when things become so dire. Be proactive about avoiding a health crisis caused by not having enough downtime.

Combine relaxing activities, self-reflection, potentially learning something new, or doing something creative—or enjoy doing nothing at all. Don't do. Just be. You'll find healing there. And best of all, you'll find your true self.

Which is exactly what Hannah did. As we write this final chapter Hannah is getting ready to head home after spending a blissful and rejuvenating break with Cassandra chillaxing in the Bay of Islands. Immersed with the sea and land, surrounded by quiet, peace and beauty, away from the pressures that had contributed to her illness she could finally heal. The life she knew had gone. The person she was had changed. She had grown, matured, and blossomed.

Prior to writing this book she had stopped singing, had no hobbies, was depressed and suicidal. She had lost her joy. Over a short period of time, weeks, in fact, her joy returned. She sang and sang and sang—and even recorded a music video with a friend who is a guitarist and filmmaker.

And she adopted a new hobby, crochet—and in the process found a new positive addiction. She put in place new mindset routines, like the Miracle Morning we shared in this book. And many, many more of the strategies we've shared in *How to Find Your Joy and Purpose.*

And, of course, she finished and narrated this book. Importantly, she'd done it all within the tranquility of adopting her new mantra, 'do less, and achieve more.'

We've both seen being crazy-busy for what it is—absolute madness!

Everything got better for us when we made peace with the fact that life might never get easier, but that in changing ourselves for the better, life also got better.

As we wrote in the Author's Note, this book is a list of things that have helped both of us—a daughter struggling to survive the aftermath of a brutal, and potentially fatal, mental health crisis; and a mother clinging to the hope and belief that helping her daughter find her joy would save her life.

We wrote to heal ourselves and in the process of recovery, we discovered how extraordinarily powerful everyday joy is for a vibrant life.

We learned how simple, quick and effective joy can be in healing the things that may otherwise slay us. The depression, anxiety, stress, lack of meaning and purpose, unhappiness at work, relationship melt-downs, suicidal thoughts, alcohol abuse, and other dis-eases were transformed.

Joy was the alchemist.

We're not saying everything is sorted. Hannah is beginning again. And many people who have written to us and shared their stories as we wrote this book, are also beginning again.

Whether due to unexpected divorces and separations, the loss of a career they'd loved, health crises, or the death of a loved one, life is a circle of endings and beginning, pleasure and pain, sadness and joy.

As trees shed their leaves in autumn, in the freshness of the new growth that follows, nature reminds us that life, if we allow it to be, is beautiful.

We wrote *How to Find Your Joy and Purpose* primarily for anyone trying to create and sustain a meaningful, healthy, and prosperous life in the wake of setbacks.

We hope you've found some helpful reminders. Above all, please, please remember to hang onto hope, follow your joy, keep going, and take care of your beautiful self—mentally, emotionally, physically, and spiritually.

We'll keep doing the same. Again and again and again.

Wishing you joy, peace, and happiness

With all our love

Cassandra and Hannah

P.S. If negative thinking or fear-based worry has you in its grip, email Cassandra for a FREE workbook from her Free to Be Me life coaching programme, *Create Your Life With Your Words Thoughts and Feelings.*

ALSO BY CASSANDRA

Transformational Super Kids:

The Little Princess
I Have to Grow
The Boy Who Cried

Mid-Life Career Rescue:

The Call for Change
What Makes You Happy
Employ Yourself
Job Search Strategies That Work
3 Book Box Set: The Call for Change, What Makes You Happy, Employ Yourself
4 Book Box Set: The Call for Change, What Makes You Happy, Employ Yourself, Job Search Strategies That Work

Master Life Coach:

Leonardo da Vinci: Life Coach

Coco Chanel: Life Coach

The Art of Living:

How to Find Your Passion and Purpose
How to Find Your Passion and Purpose Companion Workbook
Career Rescue: The Art and Science of Reinventing Your Career and Life
Boost Your Self-Esteem and Confidence
Anxiety Rescue
No! Why 'No' is the New 'Yes'
How to Find Your Joy and Purpose
How to Find Your Joy and Purpose Companion Workbook

The Art of Success:

Leonardo da Vinci
Coco Chanel

Journaling Prompts Series:

The Passion Journal
The Passion-Driven Business Planning Journal
How to Find Your Passion and Purpose 2 Book-Bundle Box Set

Health & Happiness:

The Happy, Healthy Artist
Stress Less. Love Life More
Bounce: Overcoming Adversity, Building Resilience and Finding Joy
Bounce Companion Workbook

Mindful Sobriety:

Mind Your Drink: The Surprising Joy of Sobriety

Mind Over Mojitos: How Moderating Your Drinking Can Change Your Life:Easy Recipes for Happier Hours & a Joy-Filled Life
Your Beautiful Brain: Control Alcohol and Love Life More

Happy Sobriety:
Happy Sobriety: Non-Alcoholic Guilt-Free Drinks You'll Love
The Sobriety Journal
Happy Sobriety Two Book Bundle-Box Set: Alcohol and Guilt-Free Drinks You'll Love & The Sobriety Journal

Money Manifestation:

Financial Rescue: The Total Money Makeover: Create Wealth, Reduce Debt & Gain Freedom

The Prosperous Author:

Developing a Millionaire Mindset
Productivity Hacks: Do Less & Make More
Two Book Bundle-Box Set (Books 1-2)

Miracle Mindset:

Change Your Mindset: Millionaire Mindset Makeover: The Power of Purpose, Passion, & Perseverance

Non-Fiction:
Where is Salvator Mundi?
More of Cassandra's practical and inspiring workbooks on a range of career and life enhancing topics can be found on her website (www.cassandragaisford.com) and her author page at all good online bookstores.

FOLLOW YOUR PASSION TO PROSPERITY ONLINE COURSE

If you need more help to find and live your life purpose you may prefer to take my online course, and watch inspirational and practical videos and other strategies to help you to fulfill your potential.

Follow your passion and purpose to prosperity—online coaching program

Easily discover your passion and purpose, overcoming barriers to success, and create a job or business you love with my self-paced online course.

Gain unlimited lifetime access to this course, for as long as you like—across any and all devices you own. Be supported by me and gain practical, inspirational, easy-to-access strategies to achieve your dreams.

To start achieving outstanding personal and professional results with absolute certainty and excitement. **Click here to enroll or find out more—the-coaching-lab.teachable.com/p/follow-your-passion-and-purpose-to-prosperity**

ABOUT THE AUTHORS

Cassandra Gaisford, is a former holistic therapist, award-winning artist, and #1 bestselling author. A corporate escapee, she now lives and works from her idyllic lifestyle property overlooking the Bay of Islands in New Zealand.

HANNAH JOY

Hannah Joy is a Spirit Conduit and Intuitive Healing Coach. She works with spirit to bring forward guidance, messages and insights for your highest good so that you can experience healing, empowerment, joy and live out your greatest potential.

www.hannahjoyspirit.com

PLEASE LEAVE A REVIEW

Word of mouth is the most powerful marketing force in the universe. If you found this book useful, we'd appreciate you rating this book and leaving a review.

Great reviews help people find good books.

Thank you so much! We appreciate you!

PS: If you enjoyed this book, could you do us a small favor to help spread the word about it and share on Facebook, Twitter and other social networks.

COPYRIGHT

ISBN PRINT: 978-0-9951287-7-4
  ISBN EBOOK: 978-0-9951287-6-7
  ISBN HARDCOVER: 978-0-9951287-8-1

First Edition

CPSIA information can be obtained
at www.ICGtesting.com
Printed in the USA
LVHW030818181119
637663LV00007B/2792/P

9 780995 128774